# Horseback Adventures

Also by Dan Aadland
*Treading Lightly with Pack Animals*

# HORSEBACK
# ADVENTURES

*Dan Aadland*

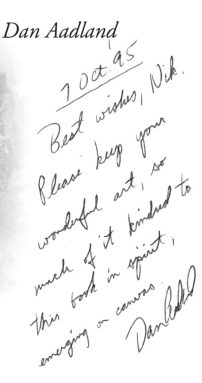

7 Oct. '95

Best wishes, Nik.
Please keep your
wonderful art, so
much of it kindred to
this book in spirit,
emerging on canvas.

Dan Aadland

Howell Book House
*New York*

All photographs by the author unless otherwise credited.

Macmillan General Reference
A Simon & Schuster Macmillan Company
1633 Broadway
New York, NY 10019

MACMILLAN is a registered trademark of Macmillan, Inc.

Library of Congress Cataloging-in-Publication Data
Aadland, Dan.
    Horseback adventures / Dan Aadland.
    p. cm.
    Includes index.
    ISBN 0-87605-925-6
    1. Travel with horses. 2. Horsemanship. I. Title.
SF285.385.A18  1995
796.5—dc20        94-48909
    CIP

Manufactured in the United States of America

10   9   8   7   6   5   4   3   2   1

*To Emily, the girl who showed me the tree burial thirty-two years ago
and then joined me for adventures on horseback and in life.*

# CONTENTS

Acknowledgments ix

1. A Gnarled Pine 1

2. Western Horsemanship: A Primer 9

3. The Ranch 35

4. Adventures on Wheels 53

5. Cattle on the Trail 65

6. Packing In 79

7. Adventures Overseas 99

8. The Endurance Trail 125

9. Solo Trekking on Horseback 137

Epilogue 165

Appendix 167

Index 178

# ACKNOWLEDGMENTS

Thanks to all who have lent me pieces of their knowledge to use in this book, not the least of whom was Emily's father, Elmer, more than anyone my bridge to our equestrian past. Robin Smith did his usual fine dark-room work in this the second book of mine to which he has contributed, and Dr. Sue and Cliff Knighton furnished the facts for the endurance chapter. Again, Emily's editorial help was indispensable.

*The author and Major.*

# Chapter 1

# A Gnarled Pine

It was just a stick, one dead horizontal stick about ten feet overhead lying across two branches of the gnarled pine in the dark coulee. I would not have noticed it, but Emily reined Brownie to a stop, and I did the same with Tommy, the big rough gelding I was riding. I looked where she pointed up into the dead pine, bereft of bark. She said, in a very quiet voice, gently, as if we mustn't disturb, that the stick was once part of the platform of a Crow Indian tree burial. "Daddy can remember when much of the platform was still there, and Grandpa could remember when bits of blanket still clung to it."

I recall vividly my feelings after her short explanation. We sat frozen on our horses for a moment, and the chill I felt was not only from the cool breeze that filtered through the pines and dried the summer sweat on my forehead. It was more than that. The years between the Indian people who left a loved one on a platform in this tree in front of me, who wrapped their family member in the best blanket they had with the best gifts they could spare, then rode their ponies silently away, the years between them and me evaporated like the wet left behind by a quick summer shower. I was suddenly very close to them and to the one whose body had returned gently to the elements from its perch in the pine.

I suppose the main reason for the closeness I felt to these people of the past was our mutual bond as human beings. In addition, I was conscious that this place had changed little if any in eighty-odd years. The sage smelled the same, and so did the pines. But would I have experienced the sudden rush of the past had I been listening to a trail bike beneath me instead of the horse that snorted his restlessness? Would the smell of exhaust instead of horse sweat have evoked the same feelings? The Crows were a proud nation of horsemen, and the sensation of sharing with them during this moment would have been far less pungent without the horses Emily and I rode quietly through the coulee.

The experience with the tree burial began a way of thinking that has never left me. To know the people and events of the past and to know the thrill of their experiences, one must form a bond. The farmer feels he knows the farmers of the past, even those of ancient Egypt. The woman who gives birth knows all her sisters from history. A man who has faced an armed enemy intent upon killing him knows, in a sense, all past warriors.

For me, a primary bond has been horses. Perhaps I didn't know that the little blond ranch girl who rode beside me would someday be my wife (though I probably suspected it), that I would live a life rarely separate from horses and, when it was, pained, that I would become a rancher who used horses in his work as well as his pleasure. I would go on to know the joys of horse packing in the Rocky Mountains, of feeling the sun in front of my tent in an elk camp surrounded by yellow aspen, the pack stock picketed nearby. I would raise horses, write of them, train saddle colts and work stock, and even in coldest Montana winter count it a poor stretch if a week went by when my foot did not touch a stirrup.

The bond with horses is not a narrow one. Until relatively recently most of human experience was intertwined with horseflesh. In war the side with the best horses had a decided advantage. Superiority of the South's horses (precursors, I'll proudly add, of the Tennessee Walking Horses I raise) was one reason for that side's early victories in the Civil War. To the Plains Indian, horses were life itself, in both peace and war, and the people measured their wealth with them. When the whites went west horses got them there, then farmed the fields so they could stay. Even in the world's great cities, horses moved what mankind needed to move, and the animals were key to his engineering feats. So when we talk of the portion of our past integrated with horses, we are talking about a sizable chunk.

The realization of the immediacy of the past, that sudden rush I felt at the burial site, has been conveyed to me by others as well. A professor during my graduate days told of a small drive of cattle entrusted to him and a friend during their teens in southern Utah. The boys delivered the cattle to a neighboring town, then returned over the desert by a shorter route. They may have known they were retracing a section of the famous Outlaw Trail, but if they did they thought little of it. They were young. That was a thing of the past.

This was still a time (the 1930s) when western travelers felt free to stop by a farmhouse and ask for a meal, so the two boys tied their horses by a small house near a corral in a desert valley. A lady met them at the door, invited them in, and fed the two cowboys at a little kitchen table. "She stared at me a minute when we first sat down, and I remember being a little embarrassed. I looked down at the black and white checkerboard oilcloth on the table. Then she said, 'It seems like just yesterday when I was drinking coffee at this same table looking across just where you're sitting at Butch Cassidy.'"

My professor experienced that same chill I felt in the coulee. Here was a woman who did not seem terribly old to him, who had served coffee to the famous outlaw at the same table in the same room, perhaps even out of the same cup, and the time for her was like the batting of an eye. And for the boy, too, the time elapsed became nothing. Suddenly his life was charged by the life of Butch Cassidy, who, like him, thirsty and hungry, had ridden his tired horse up to this ranch house and asked for a meal.

In still another time frame, Emily and I rode our horses on the route taken by General George Armstrong Custer on his way to a fatal date with destiny on the morning of June 25, 1876. With a group of mounted historians we rode twenty-three miles from the "Crow's Nest" in the Wolf Mountains to the site of that great Indian village, and while doing so we could practically hear the rattling sabers and the hoofbeats of the Seventh Cavalry that rode the route more than a century earlier. I remember the night before, lying in our tent listening to the munch of a hobbled horse punctuated by the cough of another one. A peek through the tent flap showed that our two young Walkers, short-tied to the horse trailer, were fine. But I could not return to sleep. Suddenly I realized my anxiety was normal. I was reliving an old syndrome of men on the western plains, both Indian and white, lying sheltered, trying to sleep while maintaining a vigil to guard their all-important mounts. (Some Indian braves would run a thong from the neck of their favorite horse, under the side of the teepee, then tie it to their wrists.) And then I heard it, starting to the northeast and spreading along the line of hills—the high wail of coyotes—and the feeling was complete.

It was here in the Wolf Mountains on the Crow Reservation of eastern Montana on a pine-covered outcropping called the Crow's Nest that Custer, via the hawk vision of his Indian scouts, saw a huge pony herd growing west of the Little Bighorn River. What the scouts could not see was the largest assembly in history of Plains Indians, primarily Sioux and Cheyenne, occupying a village covering some four miles of the valley bottom. And it was from here on June 25, 1876, that Custer launched the final leg of a mounted attack that left him and 264 others lying dead on the sage-covered hills east of the river.

Emily and I were there 107 years later as part of the Custer Battlefield Historical Association's re-ride and hike, a tracing of Custer's route by traveling the same ground with park service officials and historians. The re-ride was an attempt to make history live. For us equestrians, that process required not only covering the same ground, but using the mode of travel the Seventh Cavalry used, feeling the horse beneath as we traveled to the scene of the West's most famous Indian battle.

So we had driven the 140 miles from our ranch towing the brakeless, peeling two-horse trailer we owned at the time, loaded up with Emily's buckskin, Queenie, a stocky, quirky-but-smooth plantation Walker, and my Rockytop Tennessee, then at the brash and spirited age of three. (Now, eleven years later, he is *still* brash and spirited!) Tall and high-withered, Rockytop, like Queenie, was well conditioned from a spring of ranch work.

We dined that evening on a wonderful catered meal of barbecued beef, feeling almost guilty contrasting that luxury with the memory of the soldier of Custer's time, who lived in the field on a standard ration of just three items: hardtack (a tooth-breaking dried biscuit or cracker), salt pork, and coffee. On hot days the salt pork sometimes melted into a gooey mass in the middle of his pack.

The next morning we assembled with the rest of the riders on horses a little *too* eager to go. We could not exactly reproduce the Seventh Cavalry's route during the early portion of the march, for the Crow Reservation is ranched and thus fenced, and gates are not always obligingly in the correct places. But most of the time we were in sight of the ghost Seventh, across the valley. Although we came to occasional grain and hay fields, most of the countryside was traditional western range, and we speculated that Custer's men also must have passed before June green became July brown. Would the soldiers have enjoyed the ride as we were, or would knowledge of an Indian force ahead have been too sobering?

On horseback, as Custer was, we found many of the much-criticized decisions of the officer made perfect sense. Our perspective was the same as his, and when we understood his mindset, his actions, too, came clear. Custer's controversial decision to divide his troops seemed quite logical to us when we saw the terrain from the back of a horse. First, this was an officer who had considerable experience with Plains Indians, but always when they were in a *retreat* mode. He had once followed a group of hostile Cheyenne that kept splitting into halves. He had no alternative but to choose one of the trails, but that half divided again, then again, until Custer and his men caught up with a small, harmless remnant of the band. Custer's orders were to catch the Indians who had deserted the reservation (their numbers far underestimated by reservation officials), to keep them from escaping, and to do that he broadened his base by dividing his troops into three groups.

We also discovered that Custer was in visual contact with the other companies much of the time. Communication for most of the march could be by visual signals.

Another myth exploded, the one claiming Custer made a forced march that left his troops and horses exhausted and ill-prepared for battle against a fresh enemy. One of the rangers with us had ridden the route several times and said he was able to duplicate Custer's timetable (about twenty miles in three and a half hours) by alternating between a walk and brisk trot, loping occasionally. As to the freshness of Indian ponies, that is not an issue. Most of the Indian horse herd (estimated as many as 15,000 to 20,000) was grazing west of the river and missed the battle entirely. Only two dead Indian horses were found on the battlefield. The Sioux and Cheyenne fought mainly on foot and in overwhelming numbers. Hollywood has led us astray on this point.

As the day progressed it heated up, lending still more authenticity, for the thermometer on the steamboat *Far West*, tied up on the Yellowstone River nearby, registered 104 degrees on the day Custer died. Near noon we reached the "morass," a swampy area today flanked by grain fields. Here the Seventh's thirsty pack mules broke loose from their handlers, bogged down in their attempts to drink, and caused a frantic delay. We stopped too, to eat our lunches. Custer's route here is now a gravel county road. We exchanged waves with the Crow families traveling by in their pickup trucks, entertained by this group of riders, some in cavalry costume. The Custer incident is *their* history, too. Enemies of the Sioux, the Crows scouted for Custer and rode with Crook as allies against tribes they believed belonged further east. This land was already their reservation at the time of the Battle of the Little Bighorn and had been for a decade. It is understandable why they saw the Sioux and Cheyenne as aggressors. Superb horsemen and warriors, the Crows were a small tribe then. Their alliance with the whites worked well—they still live here.

For a while during that hot afternoon there was a lull in our excitement. Civilization was more in evidence—vehicles, farm machinery, and cultivated fields. But the magic returned as we drew closer. We crossed Reno Creek and entered the actual battle area and saw where Reno ran smack into the south end of the giant village, the Indians responding with a blistering attack led by Chief Gall, who lost several family members during the initial assault to bullets through his teepee walls. Reno fled with his men to a hilltop, there to make a desperate stand.

Later we dropped into Medicine Tail Coulee to parallel Custer's approach. Hidden by a ridge from the main village, he probably still was unaware of the size of the village. The coulee meets the Little Bighorn at a spot where some think Custer tried to cross, only to meet Gall and a thousand warriors. Some of the Indians claimed Custer died here and was carried up the ridge by his troops. Most, however, think Custer veered toward the high ground, eventually seeing the immensity of the force against him, and sending the final, frantic message to come quickly and "bring packs—bring packs." The packs were the mules' cargo, the extra ammunition.

As our mounted group drew closer to the ridge where Custer died we felt a tightening in our stomachs. The talkative, compatible riders grew increasingly quiet. We *felt* the great human experience, a tragedy for both sides, in a new way. I remembered reading of Curley, the teenage Crow scout who, in tears, broke the news to Captain Marsh on the *Far West*. I thought of Black Elk, the Sioux mystic who was here at age fourteen, who said that his people quit fighting, even though they almost certainly could have moved south and defeated Reno, too, because "they were sick with the smell of blood." The entire clash of two cultures, neither "good" nor "bad" but simply different, was a weight upon us as we rode the last mile. This was the last great battle of the Plains Indians, and it mobilized the whites as Pearl Harbor did in another age. As a military force, the Sioux and Cheyenne would not survive another year. Crazy Horse himself would come into the reservation and say he would fight no more if the whites would simply give his people something to eat.

The experiences on the Custer re-ride (of which I wrote in greater detail in *Equus*, December 1983) gave Emily and me a sense of those historical events we simply could not have gained any other way. But retracing the past, simulating history, is not the total story. Most Americans are descended from adventuring people, in many cases people who risked all to go to a distant land in hopes of a better life. Perhaps modern society has become too tame for many of us. Modern civilization is pretty restrictive, pretty regulated. Maybe we're a society of frustrated adventurers, descendants of those who answered the call by sailing to a new continent or building a city or homesteading land that had never been tilled.

For those of us who love them, horses seem the link to adventure. We need not seek the spiritual enlightenment of the Indian brave on a vision quest, although some do. Perhaps we're after that sense of immediacy of history I found at the tree burial or at the Custer site, but maybe we simply want to experience the beauty of a mountain meadow and the power of the moose that grazes there. Maybe we want to duplicate the experiences of our pioneer ancestors so we know better what they were made of and what we are made of. Perhaps we want to ride to the truly exotic, across an African veldt or past the castles of Europe.

In this book we'll suggest the possibilities, help you start carving out the quest for adventure that suits you as a horseperson (and I assume you're either a real or vicarious horseperson or you would not have read this far). The possibilities are varied and nearly unlimited. Most of the ones I know best can be found in the American West (though many of these have their parallels elsewhere). We'll look at life on guest ranches ranging from the plush holiday to the working vacation that guarantees calluses on your hands. We'll experience life on the seat of a wagon pulled by horses of the kind that gave civilization its muscle for centuries.

Moving cattle through a haze of dust, we will sense, through our brief experience, the life of the cowboy. We'll tackle the rough trails of the Rocky Mountains with pack animals carrying the sparse portion of civilization we need to furnish a comfortable camp by a mountain stream. Finally, we'll venture outside the American West to look for a different set of roots, those of our European beginnings, and experience the romance of riding from village to village as knights and their squires once did.

And our link to adventure through all this will be the horse, *Equus caballus,* the animal that carried mankind through peace and war and into our modern time, that has lent us its strength through the ages. As a domestic animal, selectively bred by mankind for thousands of years, the horse is a reflection both of its natural genes and of us, and its presence spices our lives and charges our batteries. Rocinante, Traveler, Trigger, Babieca, Champion—all were partners in adventure, and their cousins of today are still first choices in our own *vision quests.*

*Chapter 2*

# Western Horsemanship: A Primer

As you already know, this book has a western orientation; its author is a native Montanan, its concept touches on American Indian culture, and most of its adventures will be found in the American West. (The exception is chapter 7, "Adventures Overseas.") The American West has its own unique school of horsemanship. The school is a medley of styles found elsewhere in the world, but our horse culture probably owes more to the Mexican cowboy tradition than to any other single source.

It seems reasonable, early in this book of adventures, to give you a brief orientation in western horsemanship and in horsemanship generally. If you read, later in the book, a reference to the cinch, you will already know it is the western word for girth. (Our parent word here, in Spanish, was *cincha*.) To help the reader who is unfamiliar with *any* school of horsemanship, I'll keep the chapter pretty basic. You can learn as you go and be a little more prepared for what awaits you on that cattle drive or pack trip you're planning.

If you are an old *hand* (western for skilled helper), you may want to skip this chapter and go on to the others—but I really wish you wouldn't. I rarely talk to another horseperson without learning something new, a technique or approach, or about a new piece of equipment that might prove useful. Perhaps my discussion of western horsemanship will contain a tidbit or two useful to the more experienced.

Picture a cowboy roping the calf, a mountain man riding with his long rifle on the crook of one arm, or a modern packer leading his string into the mountains. What, in the way he rides, is different from the method of a rider following the hounds across an English landscape or that of a dressage rider in the show ring? In trying to boil western riding down into one distinct variation, I came up with this: western riding is one-handed. This is a simple but very sharp distinction. Two hands are rarely used on the reins in western riding, and the reason is simple. That mountain man we pictured earlier carried a rifle too long for a scabbard, and he had to have it constantly ready, so he rode with one hand and carried the firearm with the other. Cowboys need one hand free to swing a rope or whip. Packers need a free hand to lead their pack animals. It would be nearly impossible for me, a western horseman, to accomplish many of my everyday ranch tasks if I had to keep both hands on the reins.

These requirements gave rise to a different way of controlling the horse, of "steering" him, called neck reining. In *direct reining*, the horse responds to a direct pull on one side of his mouth. Pull the left rein and he steers left, pull the right and he goes that direction. Horses that *neck rein* are trained to respond to gentle pressure on the neck instead. The rider holds the reins in one hand and simply moves the two of them together in the direction he wishes to go. The horse feels a rein on the right side of his neck as the reins are moved left and responds by moving away from the pressure (to the left).

Of course, reins are not the only means by which we control horses. All advanced schools of riding include leg cues, that is, pressure applied one place or another on the horse's body to get a desired response. These were an important part of the Indian brave's riding skills, for he usually rode with just one "rein," often just a rope or strap looped around the animal's lower jaw. Yet, with this seemingly primitive equipment, he ran his horse among the buffalo herds and controlled him with great precision in battle. Similarly, in Spain I saw cattlemen who rode with just one rein, neck reining one direction and direct reining the other.

But that basic difference, the holding of both reins in one hand and of neck reining the horse, is an essential one, and we'll keep it in mind as we go through the photo sequence.

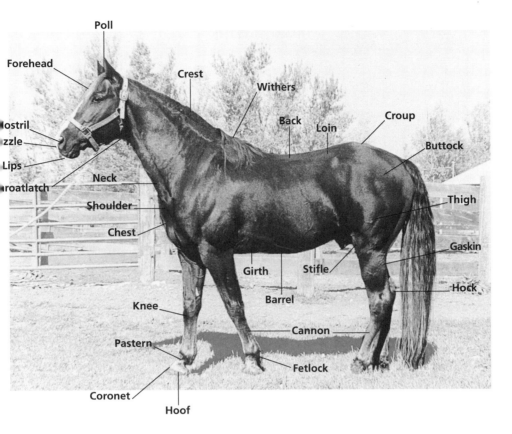

*The points of a horse as illustrated on The Pride Piper, the author's Tennessee Walking Horse stallion.*

It's a fine day, clear and fresh, our high-altitude air nice to breathe and smell. To the southwest is a front of blue mountains, and there is a scent of sage. In the corral is a gentle, western-broke horse. Never mind how he got there; he is there for you to ride. Now we are assuming, of course, that you are not going to do any of what follows without proper instruction. This chapter is a just a reminder for those already experienced and the barest beginning for those who are not. A competent instructor is a must for anyone just beginning to ride.

The animal in this corral happens to be a Tennessee Walking Horse, but that won't surprise those who know the history of horses in the West. Before the Quarter Horse became the dominant western breed earlier in this century, all light-horse breeds were represented out West, and gaited ones like the walker were quite popular. (They are becoming so again.) Any breed of horse can be western trained.

*Piper, waiting to be ridden.*

More unusual in this case is that the horse is a stallion. In the United States stallions are rarely used as pleasure or work animals, so you'll almost always be riding a mare or gelding (neutered male). The stallion pictured is extraordinarily gentle, however, usable for almost every purpose as long as the rider remembers he *is* a stallion. This one's name is The Pride Piper, and although he is fifteen years old and was trained and shown only English style, he is rapidly learning to neck rein.

Now you enter the corral, halter in hand, for you must catch the horse before you can ride it. The woman in the pictures is Emily, my wife, who is five feet one inch tall and weighs around one hundred pounds. Across the corral from her is Piper, not a large horse at fifteen hands (sixty inches) at the withers (the highest point of the back, just before the neck begins) and approximately one thousand pounds in weight. Thus Emily weighs one-tenth as much as the horse. Yet who is the dominant figure here? It better be Emily, because if it is not, we could have a disaster in the making.

Horses are big, incredibly strong animals. We must start with that fact. No horse that ever lived is 100 percent safe or foolproof. Mankind's superior intelligence, along with thousands of years of selective breeding, has created the horse as we know it, usually docile, ready to serve. But forgetting the animal's strength and basic nature for even an instant can be very costly.

And what is the horse's basic nature? It varies with individuals as much as the nature of human beings does, but it can be understood when we think in "flight or fight" terms. The horse was an open-country animal that feared predators; it was a "flight" animal. Certainly it fought sometimes, when there was no escape, for instance. Stallions fight viciously when competing for another's territory. But a horse when surprised, pressed, or harassed, will try flight as its first line of defense. Since it particularly feared predators such as the big cats, which could jump on its back, it is remarkable that humans have been able to mute that natural fear and use the animal with the rider positioned just that way—on its back.

Because horses do not like to be surprised, Emily speaks to Piper as she enters the corral. She then approaches from neither directly behind nor directly in front, but from the side, toward the horse's shoulder. This is the safest place to stand by a horse. When a horse does take aggressive action it does so by kicking to the rear or striking (and biting) in front. Another reason for avoiding standing directly in front or in back of the horse is that it actually has a blind spot in both places. Horses have bilateral vision, each eye seeing approximately half of the sphere. Seeing you clearly gives the horse a sense of security. Be especially careful when approaching horses loose in a group. Gentle animals that would never threaten you can be quite nasty with each other, and you do not want to get caught in the crossfire. Watch for telltale body language, such as ears laid back.

Emily says "whoa" to Piper, then, as she draws near, touches him gently on the shoulder. Meanwhile, she has held the halter gathered up in her right hand with her fingers clasped around the unbuckled top strap (the strap that goes around the horse's poll, just behind the ears). She passes her right hand over the horse's neck, drops the halter from her hand so that it hangs only by the top strap, then guides it with her left hand up over Piper's nose, finally buckling it. (Piper has a high head carriage and has been taught to lower his head during this process and during bridling, but Emily must stretch a little to get it done.)

Once Piper is haltered (caught), Emily ties him by his halter rope to a solid post. She doesn't merely wrap the lead rope a couple of turns around something—that was only done in western movies when there were many extras on the movie set to catch the horse when it wandered off. She ties it with a real knot, a quick-release knot traditional in Montana. (There are several variations that work as well.) Now it's time to brush and curry her horse, a process Piper seems to like. Emily also picks up and checks Piper's feet and cleans them with a hoof pick if necessary.

This handling serves two purposes. The currying and foot-cleaning help keep the horse sound and healthy, but they also renew a human touch with the animal. Yielding his feet reminds the stallion of human authority and keeps him accustomed to the manners required by the farrier when it is time for a set of shoes.

Next Piper needs a blanket or pad. While most western saddles have fleece under the tree to create some padding for the horse, a good pad or blanket is also required to protect adequately from sores. Emily lets Piper smell the pad first (not entirely necessary when the horse is well-trained), then places it farther forward than necessary, finally sliding it back into place. This step ensures that the hair on the horse's back will lie neatly down in place under the sweaty weight of pad, saddle, and rider.

Most of this work, you will note, is done from the left, called near side of the horse. The right, or off side, should not have been neglected during the animal's training, however. Along with their bilateral vision, horses seem to be of split-brain mentality. Each thing learned on the left must also be learned on the right, and a good trainer will teach a colt to be brushed, mounted, and saddled from either side. But trainers are only human. Given the press of time, many neglect to train horses equally from the off side, and you must not assume the horse assigned you by a guide or outfitter is equally safe to work from either side.

Now Emily is ready to saddle. Her saddle, made by Connolly Brothers of Billings, Montana, was purchased by her father when he was just a boy.

*Emily has caught Piper with the lead rope and will drop the halter over his neck.*

*Holding on to the poll strap of the halter, Emily has dropped the rest of the halter on the far side of Piper's neck.*

*Now it's a simple matter of bringing the noseband up and . . .*

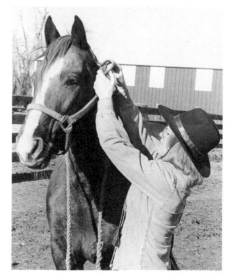

*Piper is haltered.*

The saddle is beautiful, but very heavy. Note that Emily lays the stirrup leather on the off side and the cinch up over the seat of the saddle so they'll be out of the way when she swings the saddle into position. The stirrup and cinch may fall down and slap the horse on the off side when the saddle is thrown on, but a horse should be trained to accept that.

To view Emily's old-fashioned western saddle next to an English flat saddle is a study in extreme contrast. The western saddle has a high cantle (rear), pommel (front), and is topped by a horn. The saddle horn developed primarily for roping, but it is handy for many other things also. For instance, a skilled hand can lead a stubborn horse or drag a load by wrapping the lariat (called taking a dally) once around the horn to furnish friction. When our horses must stand tied by their lead ropes (for most western work we leave the halter in place under the bridle), we tie our reins to the horn with two half hitches to keep the horse from stepping on them. When I ride in the mountains I bring the strap of my camera or binoculars up through the gullet (the open place under the horn) from the front, then put the loop up over the horn for a secure hitch. So accustomed are many western riders to saddles with horns, that they feel quite lost when they try a saddle without one.

Western saddles were built for work. They tend to be rugged, and they often distribute the weight of the rider over a somewhat larger area than English saddles, which is a plus. On the negative side, western saddles are heavier and allow somewhat less feel of the horse under you. It is harder for the horse to pick up subtle changes in leg pressure, for instance, with most western saddles. Not all are as heavy or extreme in design as Emily's saddle, of course, but I've noticed that high cantles and pommels are returning to fashion, a reaction to an era of popularity for the "pancake" western saddle with its "Cheyenne roll," a low, flattened-off cantle.

When the saddle is on Piper's back, Emily rocks it a little to find the place where it fits properly. This is hard to describe but easy to show. Saddles are made over frameworks called trees. The tree was traditionally made of wood bound by rawhide, but plastics and other materials are often used now. The two main members of the tree, pieces contoured to fit a horse's back, are called bars. The front of the bars just nudges into the place where the horse's back rises into the withers and where the back begins to widen into the shoulders. When the saddle is positioned this way it looks and feels right—at least to the experienced horseperson. The novice needs some help.

*Currying.*

*Checking Piper's front feet . . .*

*then his back feet.*

*A good blanket or pad is needed underneath the saddle.*

*The last step in blanketing is to slide it toward the rear and into place to leave the hair lying flat.*

Having made sure the cinch is lying flat against Piper's right side, not twisted, Emily reaches underneath and pulls it toward her. We like a fitting called the tackaberry, a hooked buckle over which we secure the cinch ring directly, without having to thread anything through. Then Emily draws it up snugly with the latigo, the leather strap that hangs from the left side of the saddle. Some people don't like tackaberries, and they use the tongue on the cinch ring to secure the latigo. Some westerners use neither the tongue nor a tackaberry. Instead, the latigo comes up to the ring on the saddle and is secured with a special knot for this purpose.

Since the latigo is secured with one or more loops, it acts as a block and tackle. Its mechanical advantage is considerable, so a strong person can actually cinch too tightly. The cinch should be tight enough to keep the saddle on—and no tighter. Beware of the old trick known to many senior saddle horses, that of sucking in a huge breath right before you cinch up so the cinch is actually loose later when the horse lets its breath out. Check the cinch again right before you mount.

Emily and I were raised with three-quarter rigged saddles that have just one cinch. Many western saddles locate the cinch farther forward and have a rear cinch to keep the saddle more secure while roping. (This is

*Emily secures the stirrup over the horn to keep it out of the way.*

*The saddle, ready to put on Piper's back.*

*Rocking the saddle from side to side to seat it properly.*

called full rigged or seven-eighths rigged, depending on the exact location of the cinches.) This rear cinch is always attached *after* the main (forward) cinch, and later, detached *before* the main cinch. An easy way to remember it is that the main cinch is always attached first and detached last. The rear cinch and breastcollar (if present) should never be the sole attachments.

*Bringing the cinch underneath.*

*Hooking the tackaberry.*

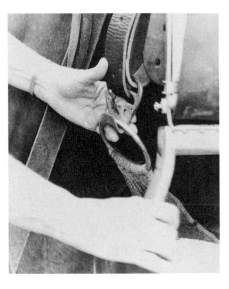

*Pulling the cinch tight.*

*This Connolly Brothers saddle, built in 1919, contrasts with an English flat saddle. The western saddle was made for hard work, the English saddle for sport and transportation.*

We don't want a horse to spook with the saddle only partially secured, and it is the forward cinch that does all the holding. The rear cinch is never buckled tightly around the horse's belly. Just take the slack out.

The stirrups of Emily's saddle are already adjusted for her, but if they were not she could quickly check for a ballpark fit by holding the stirrup out to the side while she stood beside Piper. With the stirrup at her armpit and her arm extended straight toward the horse, her hand should just touch the place where the stirrup leather joins the saddle. This is only approximate, of course. Once mounted, standing in the stirrups should make for just a hand-width of clearance between crotch and saddle. Of course, some riding styles call for shorter stirrups; jockeys ride with much shorter ones and so do the natives of southern Spain.

The bridle comes next. How bridles and bits really work is more the stuff of advanced horsemanship, but most trained horses in our area of the

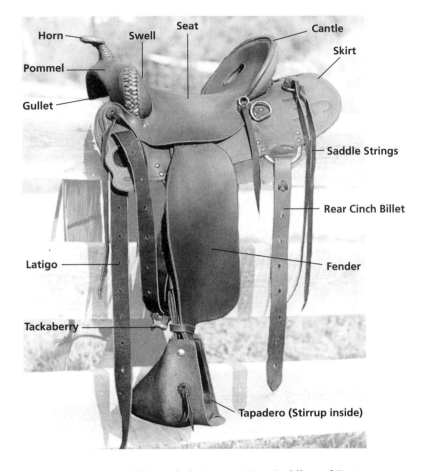

Horn
Swell
Seat
Cantle
Pommel
Skirt
Gullet
Saddle Strings
Rear Cinch Billet
Latigo
Fender
Tackaberry
Tapadero (Stirrup inside)

*A new mountain saddle made by Steppin' Out Saddlery of Ennis, Montana. The holes in the cantle allow it to double as a pack saddle, and it features D-rings, instead of just saddle strings, for tying things on.*

West are ridden with curb bits. In some parts of the West, bitless bridles called hackamores are favored. In either case, the bridle is our control module for the horse. The curb bit exerts pressure on the bars (a section of the lower jaw without teeth) of the horse's mouth, on his poll (just behind the ears), and on the under part of the jaw, from the curb strap of the bridle. Because the bridle and bit have so much mechanical advantage, we must always be gentle with the reins. Light hands are the essence of horsemanship.

*Piper takes the bit.*

*Buckling the throatlatch, or choke strap.*

We're assuming here that you already have a bridle properly adjusted for this particular horse. Don't hold the bridle in both hands and head toward your horse straight from the front. That kind of approach can scare even a seasoned animal. Notice how Emily lays her right arm on the top of Piper's neck, her hand between his ears holding the top of the headstall, then guides the bit into his mouth with her left hand. If a horse is stubborn about opening his mouth for the bit, a thumb pressed at the side of his mouth usually reminds him to do so. When the bit is in place she moves his ears inside the browband and buckles the throatlatch strap (called choke strap in our region) under his chin. The cosmetic touch is lifting the hair of Piper's foretop over the browband and smoothing it out.

Ready to mount, Emily checks the cinch again, then unties Piper and walks him around in a small circle to see that nothing is pinching, that he walks normally without the "hump" in his back that could spell discomfort and possible trouble. If Piper were a green horse, a colt just started in training, Emily would probably work him on a longe line before riding him.

Again, on his near (left) side, Emily prepares to mount. There are several ways to mount a horse. The most traditionally western way is to grasp the saddle horn with the right hand while facing forward, have the reins and a handful of the horse's mane in the left hand, then insert the left foot in the stirrup and climb aboard. However, this can be difficult with a tall horse, so Emily prefers to face the rear, twist the stirrup around clockwise, insert her foot, grab the saddle horn with her *left* hand, and swing aboard. The important thing with either approach is to keep control of the horse while mounting. It should be trained to stand still, but say "whoa" just before you mount, and keep the reins in the left hand, most of the slack taken out, the left one a little tighter than the right. Taking more slack out of the left rein will make the horse tend to step toward you rather than away should it move while you are mounting. Do not hold the reins *too* tightly, though, or the horse will think you want it to back up. Once aboard Emily makes certain she is holding the reins evenly, for if one is tight, the other loose, the horse will think you want it to turn.

At the most elementary level, most western horses respond to several fairly universal signals. A clucking sound accompanied by a tightening of the legs and touch of the heels means "go." Pulling lightly back on both reins at once, accompanied by "whoa" and a shift back of body weight,

*Ready to mount the traditional way. This method, with right hand on the horn, is the most secure, but is difficult with a tall horse. Note there is less slack in the left rein so that Piper would tend to move toward the rider if he failed to stand still during mounting.*

*An easier method of mounting for Emily involves facing toward the rear of the horse, turning the stirrup, and swinging on.*

means "stop." ("Whoa," by the way, is used *only* when you want a full stop. Novices tend to say it when they want the horse merely to slow down. I use "easy" for that, but it depends on the horse.) Sitting erect and pulling back on both reins at once, with the command "back," means the horse should step to the rear. Moving both reins to the left calls for a left turn, to the right a right turn. The horse is cued by the feel of the reins on his neck, thus the term *neck rein*.

The reins are held in one hand, but it can be either hand, and many riders switch from time to time. This will not necessarily be true if you intend to participate in western horse shows; you may be required to hold the reins in the left hand only, and the method of holding them might be prescribed as well, depending upon the breed and show class involved. (The left hand probably evolved as the preferred one so right-handed riders could do other things with the free hand.) Fortunately in most riding activities we don't have to please judges or satisfy rules—we can do what works well.

The photos show three different methods for holding the reins. The standard method is with the hand pointed forward, knuckles down, the reins coming out over the index finger. If you are riding a spirited, hard-mouthed horse that takes a great deal of holding back, you might run the reins out the bottom of your fist instead, for added leverage. (Spirited teams are sometimes driven this way.) Riding The Pride Piper, Emily prefers a couple of fingers *between* the reins (not allowed in some shows). This puts a little space between the reins so she can give a little pressure to the inside rein by turning her hand, which helps Piper make the transition from direct reining to neck reining. The same technique works well with colts when they have learned enough to move from direct reining (done with two hands) to the beginnings of neck reining.

Of course, there is much more than this to good riding. Horses may not be terribly intelligent, but they are extraordinarily sensitive, and they have tremendous memories. The memory is both good and bad. Horses retain training extremely well, but they also remember your mistakes and can quickly pick up bad habits. A confident, experienced rider invariably gets better performance from a horse because of his or her command presence. The horse knows the rider is in charge, reads the signals clearly, and performs. Sometimes a novice will then climb on the same horse and scarcely be able to make it walk.

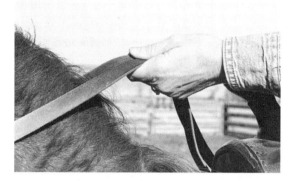

*The standard method of holding the reins.*

*Holding the reins on a hard-mouthed horse requiring leverage.*

*Getting one or more fingers between the reins allows some inside reining pressure for the horse just learning to neck rein, but this may not be permitted in some shows.*

In my memory is a graphic picture of Emily's late father, an excellent horseman, mounting a rather plain, even ugly, pinto mare. The mare was gentle, but little else could seemingly be said in her favor. But when Elmer mounted Daisy, she gathered herself, stood straighter, raised her head, and arched her neck. She looked like an entirely different horse simply because she sensed that a quality rider was aboard and that she would be expected to perform.

Riding ability like Elmer's comes only from many years of close interaction with horses. So does the subtle side of riding, the leg cue that makes the horse rein better, the feel for the correct lead when cantering, the training and skill involved with making an animal sidepass; but these are all things that will come with time. For most of the activities in this book, skill on that level is not necessary.

So Emily begins riding Piper, enjoying his quick, flat walk first. Most horses have three basic ways of going: the walk, the trot, and the canter or lope (the gallop is a fast canter). Western movies imply that horses are galloped nearly everywhere they go, but in fact, the walk and the next faster gait, the trot, tend to be used more. The walk is a four-beat gait, meaning that each foot hits the ground separately. The next up in speed, the trot, is a two-beat gait, because the diagonally opposed feet hit at the same time. The right front and left rear hit the ground, then the left front and right rear. Depending on the horse, the trot can be a pretty rough gait, so English riding developed posting, which is rising in the stirrups and sitting back down on alternate beats. Posting, when mastered, can make a rough trot more pleasant, but it is not very common out West. In the early days, saddle horses were often chosen for the smoothness of their gaits, and a reasonable trot can be ridden by supporting oneself with the stirrups, tightening the legs, and simply getting into its rhythm.

The "gaited" breeds of horses all feature gaits that are smoother alternatives to the trot. Tennessee Walking Horses like Piper have a running walk, a gait as fast as a trot but four-beat like a walk. Extremely smooth and fast, such a gait is a joy to ride. Missouri Fox Trotters, Icelandic Ponies, Peruvian Pasos, and Paso Finos all have similar fast, smooth gaits. In our part of Montana gaited horses, often called single-footers, were extremely popular in the early days, and now the gaited breeds are growing in popularity again.

After Emily enjoys Piper's flat walk, she moves him into a running walk

*Now, for the fun!*

*Starting out at a nice flat walk.*

that is so smooth she looks as if she is on a conveyer belt, then finally, a rocking-chair canter. She works to teach him neck reining and finds him very responsive. By pressing her left foot into his side when turning right, the opposite when turning left, Emily makes him associate the neck rein with the foot pressure, and he gets the idea quickly.

Before we talk about some do's and don'ts of western riding (although most of it will apply to all riding), a reminder. There are safer activities in this world than those involving horses. This may be hard to accept, but it is true. Montana, Colorado, and Washington are among the states that classify horseback riding as inherently risky. The classification was sought by horse owners who wanted the same protection against lawsuits enjoyed by owners of ski resorts. It does not mean one truly risks life and limb every time he or she mounts a horse (if that were true you probably would not be reading this book and I would not have written it). But it does recognize some realities about the nature of horses.

Second, since most of us are hobbyists where horse activities are concerned, it's unlikely we will have the skills possessed by our great-grandparents, who probably used horses daily out of necessity. We live in a fast-paced society, a mechanized society, in which few of us have the time to develop skills in *anything*, even our most treasured hobbies. How good are we at handling the tools in our basement workshops (compared to Dad or Grandpa or a professional)? How good are we at playing the musical instruments to which we were introduced as youngsters? Horsemanship is a series of skills, bound together with knowledge, and even those of us who consider ourselves experienced probably could be much better.

The truth is we rely on machines to do almost everything today. More than a century ago Emerson said that we had built a railway but had lost the use of our feet. I rely on my typewriter or computer, and my handwriting has become terrible. Most of us use pocket calculators to make up for arithmetic skills that grow increasingly poor.

Now here is the rub: Horses are *not* machines. That is a difficult concept for most beginners to accept. They expect to "operate" a horse the way they would an automobile, snowmobile, or the controls on their VCRs. Push a button and the engine starts. Kick the horse and it goes. Turn the wheel and the machine turns. Pull a rein and the horse turns. But I have never had a car try to run away because a bee stung it. I have never had my VCR try to bolt because three other VCRs ran madly by on the other side of the fence and it wanted to join them. And I've never ridden a horse so

*Piper's rocking-chair canter.*

well trained that I could sit there like a block of wood, cold, hard, and unfeeling, and have it do exactly what I wanted.

So, first we must accept that horses are not machines, that they are living, breathing creatures of flesh and blood. That makes them both wonderful and complicated. Second, we must accept that they, in their magnificent strength, are *potentially* dangerous no matter how unintentionally so. Third, let's accept that riding horses is not the world's safest activity. It's a whole lot safer than sky diving or hang gliding, activities that can make you uninsurable, but riding these creatures is not as safe as knitting.

Fourth, we should accept that a minimal level of physical conditioning and ability is necessary to be a good horseperson. Certainly this level is within reach of nearly all of us, but it does exist. At the very least, some minimum physical ability makes the activity a great deal more enjoyable.

Finally, let's accept that horsemanship is to be respected as both art and science, that although within our reach, it is not developed overnight. That concept is tough for everyone in this age of instant gratification. Have you ever seen an advertisement for guitar lessons that says, "Dedicate yourself like Segovia to a lifetime of many hours of practice each day, and you too can entertain your friends with the sublime sounds of the classical guitar"? No, we are told we can do it in ten minutes per day. The same amount of time each day will let us build a physique like that of Mr. Universe or lose the fifty extra pounds that are bothering us. But we know it is not true. Good horsemanship will require time, lots of it.

The good news is that most of the activities described in the book are within the reach of even a novice if he or she spends the time, is open to teaching, and is careful not to tackle a level too far ahead of accomplishment. Take it one step at a time. Soon you will progress from sitting on only the most docile horse to those with more pizzazz, to riding not just with your hands but with your whole body.

There is a world to learn about tack, about saddles, bridles, and bits, about the appropriate knots. Be receptive to new learning from every other horseperson you meet. Good horsemanship is far closer to good violin playing than it is to Friday Night Wrestling. Macho attitudes can hurt horses, too. Nearly every western movie shows ignorant jerks who must keep things animated for the camera, who must yank the reins instead of using fingertip pressure. An ordinary curb bit is an instrument of torture in bad hands.

Now to the do's and don'ts. Since I want to keep you out of trouble, you will see that I am heavier on the don'ts.

Do *not* ever let yourself get hung up or attached to the horse. Do not wrap a lead rope around your hand, for instance. You could be dragged if the horse spooks and runs. One of the most horrible scenarios is getting bucked off or falling but with a foot caught in the stirrup. Do ride with boots that have enough heel to prevent that and with stirrups large enough to keep from clamping your foot. Tapaderos, stirrup covers that fit over the front of the stirrup to prevent the foot from projecting too far forward, are a wonderful safety device and also protect the foot. In the unlikely event you *are* ever dragged by a stirrup, try to have the presence of mind to turn over on your belly. In that position your foot will usually come free.

You can never be too vigilant about getting hung up. When my big gelding, Rockytop Tennessee, was an extremely spirited three-year-old, I got off him in a lush hayfield to adjust something on the saddle. His head went straight down to the fine chow growing around him, of course, and when he raised his head my foot, oddly, rose at the same time. It was a feeling first strange, then terrifying. The higher his head went the higher my foot went, and in less time than it takes to tell it I had a vision of the spooky, sixteen-hand colt panicking and dragging me all the way to the Wyoming line. Just at the moment I would have lost footing on my one planted leg, whatever had caught me let loose.

In a cold sweat, I figured out what had happened. Rockytop had stuck his head down to graze near my foot, and somehow the rowel of my spur had entered the ring on his bit. As he pulled back, the angle changed, and to both his surprise and mine, wherever his head went my heel had to go. Funny now, in retrospect, this could have been a colossal disaster. Today, at fourteen, Rockytop is still too much horse for some riders, and at three he could go like a comet. Murphy's Law—"If it can go wrong, it *will* go wrong"—comes to mind. Just remember to avoid anything that could involuntarily bind you to the horse.

Should your horse try to buck or run away the control reflex is universal: Pull on *one* rein. (In the case of a runaway, I am assuming you've already tried to stop him in the normal fashion, by pulling back on both reins.) The idea is simple. A horse cannot buck well with its head up or bent around to one side. Similarly, it is usually afraid to run where it can't see. The idea is to bend the horse around and not risk pulling it over backward, which could happen if you pulled terribly hard on both reins. Normally the horse will come under control if you pull the head around with just enough force to turn it but no more than necessary. In a true emergency this would at least give you time to get off if that had to be done. More often the horse will respond by turning and quitting the objectionable behavior. Then slack off and say "whoa."

*Do* learn enough about tack to use it properly for your benefit and that of the horse. Good teachers are always best, but books and videos are wonderful too. Learn to fit saddles properly, to use bits correctly, and to care for the horse's feet. Learn enough about horse anatomy and health to recognize unsoundness or illness.

Do *not* believe that truly foolproof horses exist on the planet. Mark Twain, who got along much better with boats than with horses, claims he arrived in Hawaii and needed to hire a horse. After an unfortunate experience in Nevada, where he was tricked into buying a "Genuine Mexican Plug," he asked for "an excessively gentle horse, one with no spirit whatsoever. A lame one, if they had such." But even Mark Twain's ideal could react suddenly if stung by a bee. Learn to relax, but be ready whenever you are around horses. As your experience grows, you will learn that spirited-but-gentle, well-trained horses will teach you more about horsemanship than lazy animals will.

*Do* enjoy yourself. One of life's most sublime activities is interaction with horses. Don't let my cautions dampen your relish for the adventures that lie ahead.

# Chapter 3

# The Ranch

It was bitterly cold and the snow was deep the first time I saw the O.T.O. ranch. On a fruitless winter elk hunt, my son and I had ridden along a high ridge with occasional binocular stops to scan the breathtaking valley to the south. We could see the outskirts of Gardiner, Montana, and beyond, steam rising from the hot geyser pools at Mammoth, in Yellowstone Park. We had tied our horses by the ruins of a log cabin strategically placed as a hunting camp in a hidden coulee, a brief walk from the vantage point we used now to glass the valley. The O.T.O. had once used the cabin to accommodate their paying guests, probably for general recreation in the summer and for hunting in the fall.

But it was on the ride back, after our toes had irreversibly numbed, when cold hands made the beauty of the day harder to enjoy, when our horses' hooves squeaked with every step in the snow, that I saw the old O.T.O. buildings in a way I will always remember. Deep in another valley along Cedar Creek, nestled in aging symmetry, the now-deserted buildings of what must have once been the perfect ranch lay in quiet splendor.

What is it about the word *ranch*? Its dictionary definition is mundane enough, "An establishment for raising cattle, sheep, horses, etc., in large herds. . . ." Its parent Spanish word *rancho* gets even shorter shrift in my

*Because of scenes like this, ranch vacations are favorite family affairs. Photo: American Wilderness Experience.*

dictionary: "A hut or group of huts in which ranchmen lodge; a stock farm." This is obviously a case where connotative meanings have stronger pull than denotative ones, for if this were not so would the word be applied as widely as it currently is? There are "ranches" in South Carolina. Realtors divide agricultural land and call the fractured remnants "ranchettes," a contradiction in terms, and sell these pieces for big bucks. People with tiny properties in the West tell their friends in the city they

*There is something romantic about a ranch.*

own ranches, and those with private fortunes are currently buying Montana ranches at an alarming rate, often not to live on them but simply to own them. Once the purchase of a Rolls Royce or a Rembrandt would have satisfied the urge to own something precious; now it takes five thousand acres of sagebrush with a mountain view.

Perhaps the romance lies in the completeness of this thing we call a ranch. When we envision a ranch we do not think of the buildings only, not even only of the place. We think of a synthesis of people, animals, and setting, the smell of sage in clear air, the simplicity of interaction with cows and horses instead of bosses, boards of directors, subordinates, relatives we don't like, traffic jams, and smog. It is no wonder, then, that very early during the settlement of the American West, people figured out that there was money to be made in providing a ranch vacation for paying customers.

I could have started this chapter with a description of one of the hundreds of working guest or "dude" ranches currently operating, rather than with the deserted buildings of the O.T.O. But the ranch Jonathan and I approached, finally leading our horses (both because the way down was steep and slippery and because our blood needed stirring), was the very first dude ranch in Montana and thus deserves special attention.

Its story began with the terrible winter of 1886, a winter that killed a high percentage of the cattle on the plains of eastern Montana. Without the cattle there were also fewer jobs for cowboys such as Dick Randall. According to Jim Day, a reporter for the *Livingston* [Montana] *Enterprise*, the young cowboy looked to a source of income already surfacing in the West, that of providing recreation for tourists. He went to the outskirts of Yellowstone Park (already more than a decade old) and purchased a stage-coach and string of horses so that he could provide tours. In the fall, he used his horses to guide hunters in the game-rich mountains north of Yellowstone, especially for the elk (wapiti). Similar to but larger than the European red stag, the elk was already internationally known as a premium animal for hunters, its antlers magnificent, its meat like fine beef but with the tang of the wilderness.

In 1898 Randall had the good fortune of recognizing the owner of the O.T.O. as a stage robber in need of a quick sale and exit from the vicinity. Thus, the cowboy was able to buy the ranch. Its mountainous and rocky soil was not fertile enough to sustain the place with just crops and livestock, however. But Randall, already an experienced guide and outfitter, cultivated another kind of crop, the wealthy-but-jaded who needed a rest away from the crowd, who needed the ranch experience as a tonic. And so, for several decades, the buildings Jonathan and I looked down on that winter day were buzzing with the laughter of happy families, this day trail riding, the next fishing, the third just loafing on the porch with a good book. And, during autumn, there would have been men recounting their hunts of the day, hoping the next would bring a chance at the big one.

The O.T.O. was also the girlhood home of a remarkable woman, now ninety-six, named Bess Erskine. Her memories of life in this valley are as varied as they are stirring. Hunting grouse with a .22 revolver at age twelve, Bess faced down and killed a gray wolf that confronted her on the trail. A prized possession is a photograph of herself in a riding skirt, sitting astride a silver-inlaid saddle on a rearing horse. She can recall showing the ranch to a group of California boys who stayed for a month, one of them going on to found Douglass Aircraft. The rich, famous, and elite from the East made up the bulk of the guests that spiced her formative years.

The O.T.O. was not the only guest ranch that germinated in the disastrous winter of 1886–87. The Eaton brothers near Medora, South Dakota, entertained wealthy friends from the East for many years while

*The Beartooth Guest Ranch in Montana, a "dude" ranch in the fine old style.*

ranching times were good. Then, when that terrible winter came and wiped out their herd, they had no choice but explain to the easterners that happy as they would be to see them, they simply could not afford to keep them as guests of honor through the summer anymore, unless the guests were willing to pay something for their keep. That seemed fair enough to those who had enjoyed the Eatons' hospitality, and thus began another early dude ranch.

Although the buildings of the O.T.O. looked lonely and deserted, only the slightest feeling of nostalgia crept in as Jonathan and I rode away from them, down the creek toward the vehicles, that day. This is *not* a story of nature being commercialized by California developers, about a great ranch being splintered into ranchettes, about a Hollywood star buying a magnificent chunk of nature and locking out those who have always enjoyed it. Unfortunately, all of those scenarios are all too common in my home state today. But this is a story with a happy ending; I did not have to mourn the passing of the O.T.O. A conservation organization, The Rocky

Mountain Elk Foundation, made up of those who hunt the wapiti and care for its welfare as a species, buys tracts of winter range that are critical for the animal's survival. Pooling funds with the Montana Department of Fish, Wildlife, and Parks, this organization bought the O.T.O. and made it protected public domain. No condominiums will ever irrevocably alter this beautiful place, and *you* can go there to hike, fish, hunt, or simply absorb its beauties.

But most readers of this book will probably seek instead ranches similar to what the O.T.O. once was, because one of the most accessible horse-related adventures is a vacation on a guest ranch. Really, the whole concept is one of "having your cake and eating it too." I live on a working cattle ranch with a trout stream running right through the middle of it. I love fly fishing. How often do I do it? Perhaps once or twice each summer. Why? Because late in the day when the fishing would be good I have irrigation sets to make, or fences to fix, or hay to bale. My relatives come for a brief stay and fish more than I do in several summers.

Henry David Thoreau recognized this pleasure principle while staying at the now-famous pond called Walden. Rather smugly he told of the

*A wrangler's day starts early.*

labors of his neighboring farmers who worked and sweated and did not have time for the beauties around them. He pointed out that he gained far more pleasure from the farms than the farmers themselves, and was free of the mortgage to boot!

You have noticed that I use the terms *guest* and *dude* ranches interchangeably, but some explanation is in order. One hears the first adjective more often today, since some consider "dude" to be derogatory. It certainly was not originally meant that way. Dude simply indicated someone from the outside, usually from the East, who was unfamiliar with the culture of cows and the West. I still hear it used quite frequently by hunting guides and others as a term for their paying guests, with no negative meaning. (Quite the contrary, for the dude provides the occupation.) The more urban use of the word, meaning a man who is something of a dandy, commonly used today, was never the western meaning.

Western, horse-oriented vacations really begin with the guest ranch. The reason is the infinite opportunity to tailor the vacation precisely to

*Some want to ride like the Wild Bunch.*

*Some, through a field of flowers (the footwear of the woman in the foreground may not prevent a foot from slipping through the stirrup).*

*And some for the joy of being together. Photos: American Wilderness Experience.*

your desires. An incredible variety exists, from ranches so plush you can choose the temperatures of the several swimming pools to working cow operations where the hosts take in just one family at a time, share their home, their food, and their workday with them, giving the guests the opportunity to fix fences and get calluses on their hands if they so desire. Between those extremes are ranches that appeal to just one age group or one sex. There are ranches for die-hard equestrians who like to make riding an athletic event and for those who want to mix fly fishing, pack trips, white-water rafting, or cattle drives with the ranch stay. There are bring-your-own horse facilities offering the freedom to do your own thing with your own horses but with the logistics handled for you. I cannot think of a resort industry that allows such precise tailoring as this one.

Guest ranches allow us to enjoy the atmosphere and activities of the ranch while still keeping a foot close to civilization, and that makes them suit many families. Americans especially are pretty pampered. Parents may thrill to the idea of getting away from it all, but the children may still need an occasional television fix. Mom may still need her hair dryer, Dad his chance to swing a golf club. There is nothing wrong in admitting these needs. After all, we are after some fun, and adventure is a relative thing.

Some may need an ascent up Everest to get a charge, but for others a short ride on a gentle pony is plenty.

Let's have a look at some examples. First we will assume you really crave a taste of the life of a cowboy. You don't worry about swimming pools, golf courses, planned recreation, or the companionship of large numbers of other guests. You want to ride, learn about ranching, do some actual work (preferably as much of it as possible from the saddle), and eat genuine Dutch-oven cooking. If you can hear an elk bugle and experience some spectacular mountain country along the way, so much the better.

One of the ranches catering to such desires is Silver Spur Outfitter of Dubois, Idaho. They take no more than four adult guests at a time (children are only accommodated if an entire family books as a group), lodge them in a converted school house, and give them a taste of the working cowboy's world. Silver Spur states adamantly that they are *not* a dude ranch. They emphasize that the ranch work they do is real, not created for guests, that they host people interested in helping tend 2,000 cows in mountain country, serviced by three authentic cow camps between 7,000 and 8,000 feet in elevation. The ranch provides the horse, saddle, and all other necessities except for personal items. Cost for a six-day stint with them is a bit over $1,000.

A very different type of facility, one primarily targeting those who wish to bring their own horses, is Golden Hills Trail Rides & Resort of Raymondville, Missouri. A large operation, Golden Hills provides hookups for recreational vehicles and stalls for the horses guests bring, but will also provide horses and lodging at additional charges. Their base price includes guided trail riding, meals, use of the campground, restroom and shower facilities, a recreation and exercise room, hayrides, barn dancing, cattle driving and team penning, horse-washing facilities, and more. Not surprisingly, furnishing one's own horse and recreational vehicle makes the stay at Golden Hills considerably less expensive than at a traditional guest ranch.

Another variation on the bring-your-horse theme, this one on a much smaller scale, is The Bunkhouse Bed 'n Breakfast located in the Black Hills at Hermosa, South Dakota. A working ranch, The Bunkhouse provides rooms and a large breakfast, hay for your horse, and permission to ride the trails on their own ranch as well as on neighboring forest service land. This is a laissez-faire facility, one that leaves you to do your own thing.

Although the owners can arrange guided trail rides, they basically provide a place to stay and a lot of opportunities, some, such as visiting the tourist areas of the Black Hills, of a nonranch nature.

Some guest ranches are appealing because of approaches or settings that are unusually self-sufficient. The K Bar L Ranch of Augusta, Montana, is self-sufficient from an energy standpoint. Serviced by horses and mules only, the beautiful, rustic ranch uses hydroelectric power for electricity, naturally warm spring water for its pool, wood for heating and cooking, and teams of mules for resupply. Yet it lacks no conveniences of the sort most would want as part of their ranch experience. A radio telephone connects guests to civilization in case that is truly needed. The K Bar L serves as a base camp for pack trips into the Bob Marshall Wilderness Area of Montana, one of the world's true wonders, more than a million acres in size.

A woman who grew up on the K Bar L, Kelly Klick Hanson, operates the Castle Reef Cowgirl Camp of Wisdom, Montana. Since the two operations are associated, some parents send their daughters to the cowgirl camp while they enjoy a stay at the K Bar L. The cowgirl camp strikes me as a wonderful idea. For girls aged nine to fourteen, the camp offers equestrian instruction on all levels and has in the past limited itself to just fifteen girls for as much one-on-one instruction as possible. Taking that advantage even further, Ms. Hanson has decided to limit the number to ten in the future. Turning away extra profit to improve quality is an impressive attribute.

As one who spent many years teaching in American public schools, who saw both the triumphs and excesses of sex-equity legislation, I found Ms. Hanson's explanation of her girls-only operation refreshingly simple and direct. "I believe this camp is unique," she said. "First of all, it's just for girls. I didn't want any of my campers being self-conscious because of the opposite sex." What a fine recognition that girls need a chance to be girls, that boys need the same, in a setting free of concern with impressing the other. Anyone with a horse-crazy daughter should look very seriously at the Castle Reef Cowgirl Camp.

A horse of a very different color is the Bitterroot Ranch of Dubois, Wyoming, operated by the same Bayard Fox who is proprietor of Equitour, the agency that sets up so many horseback adventures overseas (see chapter 7). Bordering the Shoshone National Forest and the Wind River

Indian Reservation, the Bitterroot Ranch is at 7,500 feet elevation in a beautiful, remote valley. Mr. Fox raises Arabian horses on the ranch, furnishes three horses (instead of the usual one) for each guest, and appeals to a clientele of equestrians who take their horseback riding extremely seriously. "Most of our guests would be bored to tears on a traditional dude ranch," he told me. In most cases the guests are already horse people, not those looking for beginning instruction on horseback, most own their own horses back home, and most are looking for fast, exciting riding with lots of galloping. The requirement is for athletic horses, horses with endurance and speed, so Mr. Fox has chosen Arabs as the primary breed on the ranch, although his string contains a few of other breeding.

While some western riding occurs on the Bitterroot Ranch, the focus there is on lighter tack, which leaves the horses more freedom to move and to perform. The ranch has a fixture not common on western guest ranches: a full-fledged cross-country course with all the jumps and accoutrements. In discussing the tours he sets up overseas, tours that also appeal strongly to equestrian psychology, Fox says,

> *Riding is a broad term with many meanings to different people. One needs to be careful. For instance, the average dude ranch in the West does not prepare people adequately for a riding tour because they do not give lessons and the horses they use are mainly old and quiet and do not go at a fast pace. Riders are more or less passengers on their backs and are not expected to control them to a great extent. They use western saddles with a big horn to hang on to [not what the horn is for, and not even a particularly good place to hang on!], whereas most riding tours [of the Equitour type] are on English saddles. Wilderness pack trips also have little to do with equestrian ability. Real riding tours will avoid pack horses where possible because riders should not be tied to the pace of a loaded pack animal.*

In making these comparisons, Fox is talking about the *traditional* dude ranch. Many do indeed offer riding instruction on various levels, both English and western, and the Bitterroot Ranch itself offers instruction for less accomplished riders, even grouping people as to level of ability on their daily rides to the high country. But his points are certainly well taken. Although I grew up riding with western tack and have an affection for it,

*Many happy quests have passed through the gate to the Stoney Lonesome Ranch.*

I have always felt that saddles which hold the rider so securely as western saddles can also make for careless riding, riding in which the legs and seat are not called upon to do their jobs.

Noting Bayard Fox's orientation, it is easy to anticipate the kind of guest ranch he operates. He is not saying there is anything *wrong* with riding slowly, with hanging onto the horn while an old and trusty "dude" horse meanders up the trail. That can be a fine way to spend a day in nature for someone who is out on the trail for very different reasons than most of Fox's clientele. Driving a Lincoln Town Car down the freeway, cruise control locked on sixty-five miles per hour, is one type of driving; so is winding a Porsche down the switchbacks of a mountain road. It is another case of "different strokes for different folks," and we can be glad the guest ranch industry has specialized to the point that we *all* can find a place suited for us. The Bitterroot Ranch should be high on the list of possibilities for horsemen and horsewomen who wish to ride athletically, who wish to build on skills they already have.

With specialization, however, we should not lose that charm, that romance, we associate with the word *ranch*. Consider this name: Stoney Lonesome Ranch. A name such as this comes from true links to the past, links to those who came before us but share through the years a common experience with us. Neither romance nor the ring of truth comes with the pseudo-western labels realtors and developers stick on things.

Think now of a solitary young lady in Chicago nearly a century ago, laboring in a sweatshop at a dead-end job. Think of her courage in facing up to her hopelessness and taking action to end it by accepting the invitation to go west, to Montana, to a ranch to meet and marry a cowboy there. Think of the flak she must have received from her parents, her co-workers, and the ladies at church when she breathed the term *mail-order bride*. (Actually, such arrangements were common, and the marriage was normally not obligatory. If the young lady disliked the man, she could elect to work on the ranch until the expense of bringing her west was paid off.) But to those around her the step must have seemed rash indeed.

Well, our young Chicago lady *did* like the cowboy, and did marry him. (A daughter of theirs was an older lady I knew as a boy.) But the contrast between her smoggy, noisy Chicago, the din of her workplace, was almost too much. She did adjust, but a wonderful touch of her outlook comes through in a name she gave her home. This, she said in her letters back to Chicago, was her stony, lonesome ranch.

Now, many years later, see this cabin restored as a place where visitors from the East and Europe can have a chance to experience the aura of a ranch. This restoration should not have been made by someone outside the culture of the West, however. Far better that it was made by a real Montana ranch couple, Corky and Clarice Hedrick, people who have known struggle with drought, disastrous cattle prices, physical challenge—all things *real* ranch life includes. Late in their careers as ranchers, the Hedricks have found a different kind of productivity on their mountain ranch, something different for their land to offer. They take in guests who want to know about Montana ranch life, and they love doing it.

While they also pack people into the mountains and take them hunting in the fall, the Hedricks' true forte has emerged with a clientele who want to actually work on a ranch, who wish to get blisters and feel trail dust cling to the sweat on their faces, who wish to dig postholes and stack

*Corky Hedrick and the Stoney Lonesome Cabin.*

hay. Their guests are adamant about one thing: they do *not* want a Hollywood version of the West. They want the real thing.

During the summer of 1994, 140 guests passed through and back out the gate of the Stoney Lonesome Ranch. This, Clarice tells me, was too many. Like many businesses with sudden, stunning success, the temptation was to take on a little too much, and the ranch will be throttling back to a level of visitors it can handle without so much help and with greater satisfaction. Ten at a time is about right, Clarice feels, and they will hold it to that in the future.

Visitors, during the summer of 1994, came from all over the United States and from Denmark, Germany, and England. Many stayed longer than their original booking. The man from Denmark had booked for eight days and stayed four weeks. He did every conceivable job the Hedricks could find for him, relishing each and showing up early for breakfast to see what lay ahead for the day. Since the Hedricks like to give a full cultural experience to foreign visitors, they took him also to a baseball game, the only thing he did not like. He had not come to Montana to see a stadium crowd watching a game he did not understand. There were postholes to dig! Corky gets teased by his neighbors about having paying guests to do such work, but the same old principle is in order—it is only work if you *have* to do it, and the Hedricks have gained a new appreciation for the beauties of their ranch and of their lives by seeing the joy others take in them. Sometimes we all need a nudge in that direction. Anyway, as one who stacked hay near the Hedrick ranch as a boy, I saw Corky work so hard I can only be happy he gets a chance to spend more time in the saddle today, escorting his guests. He was, I thought, one of the most powerful men I had ever seen. I watched him jump from the top of a haystack, swing on the tooth of the tractor loader about twelve feet up, then drop gently to the ground.

Though over sixty, Corky is *still* a powerful man, fit and tanned, the epitome of one who has lived his life outdoors. He put on a pot of coffee as he talked to me one day, eyes shining when he recalled his growing up on their hilltop ranch. His father used to buy teams of horses too unmanageable for the beet farmers in eastern Montana. His retraining program consisted of a hard winter feeding hay. By spring the teams were more docile, so he would sell them at a profit. Corky's father raised mules, too, running giant jacks with a string of fifty work mares to produce big mules to export south to the cotton fields. Sitting across the table in the kitchen of their rustic ranch house, Corky exudes enthusiasm for his way of life, his work, his newly found "crop" of appreciative ranch guests. But his boots are planted too firmly on his ranch soil to quit caring that cattle prices are falling, that government regulations are making ranching more complicated. He still feeds his cattle with horses through the winter. Perhaps the additional money brought in by his guest operation would cause some men to find a more mechanized way, but I doubt whether that will happen with Corky. His life is too intertwined with horses.

Meeting wonderful, appreciative people is one of the best parts of the guest operation according to Clarice. Certainly there has been some culture shock, some adjustment to the fact that guests often do not know even the most fundamental things about livestock and ranch life. But I could tell how much Clarice was really enjoying herself when she told me, "It's all in the hospitality. If you meet them with a handshake and a grin, and if they smell cookies or pie baking when they walk in, you've got them for the whole stay." If she and Corky have any regrets so far, she said, it is only that they did not start taking in guests years earlier.

So the future of the Stoney Lonesome Ranch seems secure indeed. Bookings for next summer include hosting an entire family reunion, entertaining a group of school children from Georgia who will take an environmental class in the form of a backpacking trip with the ranch as base camp, and escorting two photographers from *The New York Times*. The requirement laid on the Hedricks by the photographers was at once simple and intriguing. "Take us," they said, "up high on a mountain where we can see a really beautiful sunrise." That is an easy assignment for Corky. He knows just the place, and he's champing at the bit to get them there.

# Chapter 4

# Adventures on Wheels

Not long ago I enjoyed hosting a family reunion at our ranch in Montana. A highlight was to be a hayride for the entire extended family, forty-odd people. I was confident in my young team of Belgians, Poncho and Lefty, but as host a bit apprehensive, too. My sons had built front and rear racks for our twenty-foot flat-bed trailer. We had hitched it to the forecart and pulled it on a practice run with the team. But this was the real thing. People were looking forward to this, and I would be asking the horses to pull a gross load of 8,000 to 9,000 pounds. I sneaked away from a game of volleyball a bit early. Middle son Jonathan helped me harness the horses, currying first, then giving them a generous feeding of rolled grain. They would need it. Then, when the time came, I put on their bridles and tied a lead rope across their rumps to keep them close together while I ground-drove them to the hayrack. (When they are older and better trained, this step will not be necessary.) Then I guided them toward the tongue, asked Lefty to step over, and backed them into place.

The steps in hitching are critical. As always, Jonathan and I snapped the neck yoke into place first, which lifted the tongue so that it would not catch on the ground in case the team moved off. Poncho and Lefty stood like rocks, however, with Emily holding the reins from her seat on the forecart. We attached the tugs on the rear of their harnesses to the single-trees. They were ready.

I mounted the forecart and called the horses' names, then clucked to them. I wish I could say they lowered their heads in unison, laid into the harness, and quietly moved us off, but it was not quite that simple. Lefty, the quicker of the two, lunged ahead of Poncho and bounced back to the rear at the very time Poncho put his two thousand pounds into the collar. Unaided, he too failed to move the load alone and eased off just when Lefty lunged. Like two clowns in a narrow doorway, they hemmed and hawed, the human cargo on the trailer growing silent and concerned. Actually, perhaps only ten seconds passed before the horses did what all good teams, horse and human, must do: pull together. Then we moved off down the lane and over the bridge, the people resuming their chattering but awed, too, at the power under those sorrel hides.

In an age when automobile travel seems slow to us, when Europe is but hours away, when tremendous machinery builds up and tears down, the term *horse and buggy* is assigned to the slow, the old-fashioned, the ineffectual. Because we have replaced animals in harness with other kinds of power, we have lost touch with just how efficient and powerful draft animals are. More, we assume modern civilization really got going when horses in harness were replaced, but really the reverse is true. Some historians consider the invention of the horse collar, the innovation that allowed true efficiency in transferring four-legged power to pulling a load, the breakthrough that made civilization advance.

Take a look around you. Nearly anywhere you might live you are likely surrounded by things built not by backhoes and bulldozers and dump trucks but by horses or mules in harness. That railroad grade was probably originally made by teams of horses and muscular men, the horses pulling a device called a "slip" that looked a bit like a wheelbarrow without the wheel. A metal box with a sharp front edge and two handles to the rear, the slip moved dirt or gravel. Most of our original roadbeds, irrigation ditches, and canals were built with it.

Look at that beautiful church (or home or office building) built before World War I. How were its foundation stones hauled? How was its timber brought to the site? Again, the answer lies in the work team. And when we look at the westward expansion of our nation, even after the first railroads

*George Miller, 83, and Dorothy, wagon masters.*

were built, we have a history of millions of tons of humans and their possessions moved west by the muscle of horses, mules, and oxen. Throughout the West today it is easy to find ruts left from the Oregon, Santa Fe, Bozeman, and Mormon trails.

Most American families can still tap Grandma or Grandpa for a recollection of a day before tractors eclipsed horses, even if the recollecting is secondhand. My father recalls, when a small boy in Stavanger, Norway, seeing teams of immense Belgian horses pulling high-wheeled carts up the city streets after a deep snowfall. Crews of men walked alongside shoveling the snow into the wagons.

Later, when he was a young Lutheran pastor on the plains of North Dakota, Dad miscalculated and steered his car into a bottomless snowbank on a farm. He looked around in despair. A tractor was parked nearby, but he found it hard to believe the small machine could do much with his car, which was practically buried. The farmer came out, looked over the situation, then said solemnly, "I guess I'll have to get the horse."

"The horse?" Dad thought. The man must be kidding. But soon he emerged from the barn with a harnessed Percheron. The farmer attached a chain from the single-tree to the front bumper, while Dad circled to the rear to push from the back for whatever it was worth.

"No," the farmer told him. "You get in and steer." My father, incredulous, took his place behind the wheel, then got a typical lesson for modern, urban Americans when they first experience the power of a draft horse. The animal simply leaned into the collar, just leaned and started walking, and the car lifted gently out of the snow and back onto the road.

Most people today would look at a draft team and think two horsepower were represented there. They know their *lawnmowers* have more power than that. But the horsepower rating was created to approximate a continuous level of power a horse could supply. In fact, draft teams at pulling contests sometimes register, when put to a dynamometer, more than thirty horsepower for short distances, and this is drawbar horsepower, not comparable with engine horsepower. Further, draft horses have tremendous traction. All four feet dig in. On muddy ground there would be no contest between a team and a small tractor.

But an even greater reason draft horses are still loved by so many is a thing we could call *soul*. Milkmen were among the last to give up their horses in American urban settings. What machine could be taught the milk route, would stop automatically at the doorstep of Mrs. Brown and Mr. Granger? What truck would make all the correct turns on the way home, leaving the milkman to his quitting-time thoughts? On the farm, work horses became, literally, members of the family. When one died it was not uncommon for the children to stay home from school for a couple days. An old and trusted friend had passed on, and they needed time to recover.

A Hungarian immigrant once stopped by our ranch and told me he had lately become interested in horses. "I should always have been interested in them, though, because I wouldn't be here if it hadn't been for a horse." The story that followed was fascinating. During World War II, this man, as a small child, was riding in a wagon laden with two families and all the possessions they dared take, fleeing in front of the enemy army, the wagon pulled by a huge, lone horse. In the middle of the night, during a terrible snowstorm, the horse suddenly stopped and refused to go on. Thinking the horse was merely tired, the driver used the whip. The horse

*The author at work.*

stayed resolutely still. Finally the driver waded through the snow and discovered they had somehow lost the road. The horse stood at the brink of a cliff, an inky blackness ahead.

I grew up with many similar stories, usually originating from the plains of the Dakotas and eastern Montana where whiteout blizzards are common in terrain devoid of landmarks. The horse's incredible sense of direction, his homing ability, was often celebrated in these. We often heard sad stories, of families found frozen in their wagons, the horses virtually parked on the porch of the farmhouse, the people never having known the horses had brought them home. Nor can any lover of Tolstoy forget the magnificent horse in "Master and Man," the one who after the blizzard has died, literally, on his feet.

All who love horses miss an entire dimension of their favored world if they never know horses in harness. To renew touch with draft animals can also give flashbacks into our past even greater than those we get when interacting with saddle horses. The meat and potatoes of civilization were moved in wagons pulled by these gentle, purposeful animals.

It is not surprising, then, that wagon trains have become a favored recreational activity in the American West. The advantages of this kind of horse-related recreation are many. The pace tends to be a bit more relaxed than that of a pack trip, and the wagons themselves form quite a support system. A full camp kitchen is normally housed in one wagon, and there is sleeping space in the others. More luxuries can come along when everything need not be packed on an animal's back. After all, covered wagons were the first recreational vehicles. Long after the true need for them passed, such vehicles were used for camping trips and fall hunting expeditions.

Perhaps the greatest advantage of a covered wagon vacation is that one need not be physically able to ride a horse in order to enjoy a wonderful equine experience. A good friend of mine, late in a life intertwined with horses, though suffering the effects of a terrible automobile accident, still enjoys himself greatly. He has taken up *driving* rather than riding horses.

Wagon trains are accessible to the aged, the very young, the handicapped, those too heavy to ride, and those who just feel insecure with the thought of being mounted on a horse. Yet occasional horseback riding is often offered on wagon trains, so the best of both worlds is possible. One can ride a portion of the day, mount the wagon for part of it, and top the day off with a brisk walk alongside to get the circulation going.

More than anything else, recreational wagon trains exude *fun.* They involve people of all ages, something too rare in our society. They are eminently *social,* the movement along a route the only real task, the rest being shared experiences, eating, camping, tending the stock. Emily and I rode along one day recently on a small wagon train traveling from Red Lodge, Montana, on a semicircle to eventually terminate in the town of Absarokee. Traveling over graveled county roads at the foot of the Beartooth mountains, the wagons moved at a surprisingly brisk clip. At least as many people rode horseback as occupied the wagons, and everyone seemed to be having fun.

We had asked octogenarian wagon master George Miller to let us ride along for a day and photograph the activity, and he was more than accommodating. "Come for as long as you want, ride anywhere you want— we're glad to have you." Since photos were our prime objective, we spent most of the morning shifting our Tennessee Walking Horses into a running walk, passing the wagons, finding a strategic spot, and photographing everything that went by. This we did several times. My horse Major

*Wagon trains are family affairs.*

had his reservations about passing squeaking wagons, especially those pulled by mules, so I got an occasional snort and sidestep.

Organization of this group was laissez-faire, the wagon master's position at the front of the train the only real evidence of structure. Horseback riders went on ahead when they wished. A pickup truck pulling a flatbed trailer carrying portable rest rooms magically appeared at rest stops, and we had noticed earlier, at the campsite, a neat stack of hay for the horses.

These things indicated the best sort of leadership, the kind that gets things done without making a lot of waves. When I complimented Mr. Miller later on the morale of the group, he was pleased. "I have my organization, but I keep it behind the scenes as much as I can. People come on these trips to feel free, and they aren't happy with a lot of warnings and rules. If they want to do something I think might be dangerous, I tell them how I feel, but other than that I let them do their own thing. I suggest things rather than try to order them."

George Miller is not a professional outfitter. He organizes wagon trains for the sheer joy of it, so most of his participants are folks who own horses and wagons and love spending part of the summer on such treks. Logistical costs are simply divided up on a per-person basis. His trusty team of gray Percherons have become a very familiar sight all over Montana. This particular trip was near the still-visible tracks of the Bozeman Trail.

George has been organizing wagon trains for over a decade, but his roots in draft horses go back much farther. "I logged with horses for twelve seasons," he told me, "and I used to train teams professionally." I could tell by his tone that one of his proudest accomplishments was during the winter of 1938. Starting in January with just one gentle draft horse, he faced a herd of Percheron/cayuse crosses aged three to eight, the object being to produce gentle work teams for farming. By the end of April he had trained five four-horse teams and one three-horse team, a Herculean task.

The day we rode along, George was leading a small but interesting wagon train. There were several teams of horses pulling conventional-looking covered wagons, a mule team pulling another, a second mule team pulling a large surrey, and a single horse pulling a buggy. The man with the buggy told me he had restored the vehicle, virtually rebuilt it. Only a few of the original parts remain. His granddaughter sat happily by him on the spring seat.

Most who gravitate toward wagon train vacations, however, will not travel with a self-outfitted train like George Miller's but will book with one of the many outfitters offering a complete service, who furnish all equipment except personal gear. An example of the many companies offering this service is Wagons West, of Afton, Wyoming. Their wagon trains travel under the spectacular vista of the Grand Teton mountains in Wyoming, backdrop for the movie *Shane* and dozens of others. The folks

*Scenes from George Miller's wagon train.*

behind Wagons West have been pack trip outfitters for years but realize that "many people wish to have a genuine outdoor experience but cannot spend the time or do not feel qualified to undertake such a strenuous expedition." Thus they developed wagon train treks tailored to the American lifestyle. These range in duration from two days and one night to six days and five nights. Several options are available: Guests can ride in the wagons the entire time, ride half the time on a gentle horse, or do the entire thing on horseback. Meals are cooked over an open fire in Dutch ovens, a western tradition, and guided side trips are available.

A Wagons West trip starts with your arrival in Jackson, Wyoming, the day before the scheduled trek. The next morning you are transported to the staging area to meet the wagon master and fellow guests and to be assigned a wagon and saddle horse (if applicable). Your sleeping bag and other gear will be stowed in a wagon, and you'll begin a jaunt through the Bridger-Teton National Forest. Costs for all this in 1994 ranged from $260 per person ($220 for those under sixteen) for the shortest trip, two days and one night, to $675 ($550 under sixteen) for the six-day, five-night expedition. There is an extra charge if you wish to ride a saddle horse the entire time (instead of just half each day), and there is a discount on trips for large parties. There are, of course, several additional firms, listed in the appendix, that offer similar adventures.

History buffs seem especially attracted to wagon trains, and with good reason. According to Harry Sinclair Drago in *Roads to Empire: The Dramatic Conquest of the American West*, in the twenty-five years preceding the completion of the first transcontinental railroad, 300,000 people went west over the Great Plains. Think of the myriad human dramas there, the dreams fulfilled, the dreams shattered. There are graves along the Oregon Trail, many of them. In that high dry stretch in Idaho, within sight of the inaccessible Snake River far below, there was once a shattered junkyard of fractured hopes. Grand pianos, rosewood dressers, carved furniture of all sorts were jettisoned when the water ran out, when the teams of horses, mules, and oxen were pushed to the limits of muscular endurance and the load had to be lightened.

On the flat above the foothills east of my house, above the pine coulee I described in chapter 1, the coulee with the tree burial, there is what looks like any two-track jeep road today. But it is a spur of the Bozeman trail, the trail opened by a quiet fellow named John Bozeman, who left his

62

*A girl enjoys riding in a buggy rebuilt by her grandfather.*

legacy in this trail and the Montana city named after him. Bozeman and the famed Jim Bridger laid out rival trails with similar purposes, to supply the growing Montana mine fields. But the Bozeman Trail was short-lived. Originating in southern Wyoming and proceeding northwest into Montana, the trail was the source of a bitter dispute with the Sioux Indians under Red Cloud. By 1868 Red Cloud and his warriors, with slashing guerrilla tactics, had effectively closed the Bozeman Trail, stopping the white man's attempt to take what they considered their land, land that, ironically, they themselves had recently taken from their enemies, the Crows.

The conflict left behind the bodies of warriors of both sides, killed in battles such as the Wagon Box fight and the Fetterman fight. John Bozeman himself died at Indian hands during the spring of 1867. According to his partner, one Tom Cover (quoted in Mark Brown's *The Plainsmen of the Yellowstone*), the two were camped in Montana at the mouth of Mission Creek when five Indians approached with their hands signaling peace, saying they were "Ap-sar-ake," Crows, friendly to the white man. Suddenly Bozeman remarked, "I am fooled; they are Blackfeet. We may, however, get off without trouble." But that was not to be. The Blackfeet leader pulled a musket from under his robe and fired, "the ball taking effect in

B.'s right breast, passing completely through him. B. charged on the Indians but did not fire, when another shot took effect in the left breast, and brought poor B. to the ground, a dead man." Tom Cover was wounded himself, killed one of the Indians, and managed to escape.

As to Red Cloud, in successfully closing the trail he won a war with the United States. The treaty of 1868 acknowledged that and infuriated senior army officers and others who knew that Red Cloud had negotiated for land traditionally held by the Crows and Shoshone rather than the Sioux. No matter, for the treaty was soon broken by both sides anyway. Red Cloud himself rested on his laurels a bit. He retired, refused to join Sitting Bull, Crazy Horse, and the others who eventually did in General Custer, and would come to be contemptuously called by those Sioux still hostile a "hangs-around-the-fort" Indian.

A few years ago a wagon train retraced the Bozeman Trail. Such reenactments of history by wagon have become relatively common, but they are task organized, not regularly held for the most part, so advance information is a little harder to find. Contacting the tourist bureaus of the western states and outfitters offering wagon trips should yield information about proposed historically oriented trips. There is nothing that gives a greater sense of our American past than holding the reins of a work team from the seat of a wagon heading west.

# Chapter 5

# Cattle on the Trail

For his wonderful 1908 book *The Log of a Cowboy*, Andy Adams chose an epigram from a source used by writers from Shakespeare to Hemingway, Chaucer to Bradbury, the Bible. It is, simply, this: "Our cattle also shall go with us" (Exod. 10: 26). As is true with many simple things, the quotation is deceptively powerful. A captive people is being held by a tyrant who continually breaks his promises to free them. Late in the "negotiations" the quoted statement is said with great finality. It is not a request, but a powerful statement of fact, an in-your-face assertion.

My mother was born in Madagascar, where her parents were Norwegian American, Lutheran missionaries. She told me tribesmen measured their wealth in cattle, that it was as improper to ask a man how many cattle he had as it is to ask someone his or her bank balance today. The cattleman I met in Spain was bold enough to ask how many cows I had in Montana, but polite enough to receive the information stoically, without comment.

To those of us in the Judeo-Christian tradition, our past as herdsmen, as nomads who followed our livestock from place to place, searching always for grass, is exceedingly close. Until this century, nearly everyone across small-town America still had livestock. The banker, the minister,

*Major's view of the Aadland herd moving down a fence line. It doesn't take many cattle to stir up dust.*

the doctor—virtually all had chickens in the backyard and a piece of pasture outside town. The vegetable garden and a small contingent of livestock were simply part of self-sufficiency.

Now, of course, too many in our urbanized society think of food as originating in the supermarket, in colorless plastic containers. We are told that the same food which allowed us to survive and thrive as a species is bad for us, that grazing ruins the ground, that the life of any living creature is equal to our own and that we therefore must not take it for food or leather. Some even complain about the use of wool. (Oddly, other predators in nature are not similarly criticized for *their* use of the food chain.)

The sense, too, of bonding with the animals that give us life is gone from many people. They have difficulty understanding a cattleman's reservations about the stocking of wolves in my part of the world, for instance, and feel an offer to compensate him financially for livestock losses

*Jonathan and Emily push cattle across our bridge.*

*It's tough to push cattle through succulent alfalfa.*

*Crossing the East Rosebud River. Some always find their way to the wrong side of the fence.*

should end the concern. Such people have never left a warm bed in the middle of a winter night to help a heifer give birth to a calf. More than money is involved. The cattleman's concern goes back thousands of years, to the protection of one's flock, a metaphor for centuries of our cultural tradition; the concerns of his critics are extremely recent ones by comparison.

But others in our modern world have yearnings in the opposite direction. They wish to touch the roots of our herdsman past, to smell the trail dust, to listen to the bawling of cows and calves, to "head 'em up and move 'em out." This chapter is for them.

I am especially fond of Andy Adams's book, because it is one of the few written by an actual trail cowboy. Cowboys, like mountain men, were not a particularly literate sort. A few from each group wrote their memoirs, but cowboys left that job largely to fiction writers, the producers of "dime novels," people who messed up the job pretty badly. Many such writers were easterners with no cowboy experience. In their favor, they elevated the West of the late nineteenth century to epic heights and made the cowboy's life *the* western experience in people's minds, even though the American West was equally dominated by the mountain man, miner, homesteader, and Indian.

It was while reading a ridiculously unrealistic depiction of life on the cattle range that Adams decided to try his hand at writing an account. *The Log of a Cowboy* is not a nonfiction narrative of one actual drive Adams took, but rather a composite of several in his experience. Realists will argue with some of what Adams gives us, pointing out, for instance, that Adams censored the language of the average cowboy to suit Victorian sensibilities. Perhaps, but attempts to learn about cattle driving as it actually was still invariably begin with *The Log of a Cowboy*.

The first few pages of the book tell us why Adams chose the quotation from Exodus as his epigram. During his boyhood in Georgia the Civil War was raging, and a small bunch of cattle was the family's only resource. The herd, consisting of just two yoke of oxen and three milk cows, was given to the protection of the boy, who hid them daily from Sherman's soldiers. The customary bells had been removed, but one ox was belled at nightfall so the herd could be easily located early in the morning. It was the boy's job to remove the bell each morning, and he carried it stealthily back and forth, stuffed with grass to muffle it. More than once, from his

*Checking the brush.*

hiding place in the brush, Adams watched soldiers pass, once nearly losing his cattle when the grass fell out of the bell and it tinkled.

After the war the family moved to Texas, and the life of a cowboy began. But the massive cattle drives of the 1880s require some historical explanation, with the great grass country of the Dakotas, Montana, and Wyoming and several historical events being key. Early settlers had seen little value in the tall grass of the northern plains. They were geared to cultivation, and dry-looking grasses, brown in late summer, seemed part of a western wasteland. What they did not know was that these waving grasses, these grasses that nourished millions of bison, were extraordinarily high in protein. Discovery of their potency came gradually.

Impoverished parties sometimes turned out their livestock to die, not believing the animals could survive the winter, then recovered them months later in better condition than when turned out. Someone discovered that a three-year-old steer, mature in Texas, would grow and gain several hundred pounds when moved to the ranges of eastern Montana. Young saddle horses, having reached their mature size further south, would resume growing when transported north, actually increasing in height by a full hand (four inches).

As the fame of the northern grasslands grew, investors, foreign and domestic, realized there was money to be made in the cattle industry. Young steers could be bought in Texas and Mexico, driven to the northern states, grazed there for a season, and sold at immense profit. However, three historical changes had to occur first. The "Indian problem" had to be settled; the bison, wild bovines competing for the same feed as cattle, had to be removed; and a way of getting beef to market had to evolve. Through some dramatic and admittedly sad changes in the late nineteenth century, all three things came to pass. The Indians were put on the reservations, the buffalo were processed to near-extinction, and the railroad penetrated into the tall grass country so cattle could be sent to the great markets of Chicago.

The first of these developments, the sad plight of the Plains Indian, was directly related to the cattle drive in another respect. The treaties that put the tribes on reservations often agreed to furnish the Indian people with massive quantities of beef to replace the bison meat they might have had if their way of life had continued uninterrupted. Truthfully, the Indians considered beef a poor substitute for bison. They called beef "soft meat," in the belief that a diet of it made one's muscles soft, while bison was "hard meat." We might suspect the difference lay in the way each type of meat was acquired. The chase of the buffalo made one's muscles hard, while having beef delivered at government expense did little for physical conditioning.

To support the northern reservation with cattle during this era, the government contracted delivery of massive herds on the hoof. The herd in *The Log of a Cowboy* numbers 3,200 head of range cattle assembled in northern Mexico, destined for the Blackfeet Indian reservation in northwestern Montana, next to the Canadian line. As the crow flies, this was twice the distance from Chicago to New York and nearly equal that of

Chicago to Los Angeles. On the ground, detouring terrain that was impassable, the miles multiplied. The logistics were staggering. There were rivers to cross, deserts where the animals' tongues would swell for lack of water, and other herds to meet or pass through (imagine the difficulty in keeping them from mixing).

The demands on men and horses were tremendous. Each cowboy was issued a remuda of ten horses, often chosen on a rotational basis, the foreman claiming the smooth-gaited ones. Those who cared for the horses well found this adequate; those who were careless in caring for them were poorly mounted at the end of the drive. The psychology regarding the importance of horses was simple: A man on foot was worthless.

For the cowboys, 3,200 cattle lined out on the trail must have been an incredible sight, if they could see at all through the trail dust. On our small ranch we occasionally trail eighty cow/calf pairs. Under dry conditions even such a comparatively tiny herd can stir things up considerably. Adams pictures it for us:

> On the morning of April 1, 1882, our Circle Dot herd started its long tramp to the Blackfoot Agency in Montana. With six men on each side, and the herd strung out for three quarters of a mile, it could only be compared to some mythical serpent or Chinese dragon, as it moved forward on its sinuous, snail-like course. Two riders, known as point men, rode out and well back from the lead cattle, and by riding forward and closing in as occasion required, directed the course of the herd. The main body of the herd trailed along behind the leaders like an army in loose marching order, guarded by outriders, known as swing men, who rode well out from the advancing column, warding off range cattle and seeing that none of the herd wandered away or dropped out.

Working cattle is basically applying pressure where you do not want the cows to go, leaving them free to progress where you do want them to go. The less pressure used, for the most part, the better. Adams's foreman put it this way:

> Boys, the secret of trailing cattle is never to let your herd know that they are under restraint. Let everything that is done be done voluntarily by the cattle. From the moment you let them off the bed ground in the morning

*Moving cattle through mountain timber. Photo: American Wilderness Experience.*

*until they are bedded at night, never let a cow take a step, except in the direction of its destination. In this manner you can loaf all day, and cover from fifteen to twenty miles, and the herd in the meantime will enjoy all the freedom of an open range.*

On these early, massive drives the herds became hardened to the trail and were able to graze enough to stay in condition while walking. The cattle of the time, however, were often as wild and quick as deer. Stampedes were always a worry. Fear can escalate like wildfire in any herd animal, and when a stampede occurred, usually at night, there was nothing to do but ride like the wind along with the animals, trying everything including pistol shots in the air to turn the front animals. When the stampede was over there was a roundup of the herd and another elaborate count, the animals herded slowly in a column between pairs of cowboys, each counting with his own system for keeping a tally.

The days of these great cattle drives are gone forever, of course. There is simply no economic reason why so many cattle would ever be moved so far on the hoof. But the working of cattle, moving them from pasture to

*A cow camp with range (teepee) tents pitched. Photo: American Wilderness Experience.*

pasture, remains an integral, necessary task in the West. Some ranches do move extensive herds to summer pasture in the mountains each spring, then back in the fall. Such summer pasture is often public land, usually administered by the U.S. Forest Service. (This tradition could also disappear if political forces that want all cattle off public land prevail.) Even ranches without mountain pastures normally require a fall roundup to gather the pairs and wean the calves.

There have been some extensive trail drives held for commemorative purposes. One of the biggest was the Montana Centennial Cattle Drive in 1989, held on the one hundredth anniversary of Montana's statehood. Progressing from central Montana south to the city of Billings, the drive was a wonderful, lengthy party, with country singers entertaining by the campfires at night and a whole wagon train of logistical support following behind. There was an extensive herd of cattle involved, large enough to keep things realistic. People who shared the drive look back on it now with nostalgia and share a pleasant camaraderie.

Moving cattle requires a bit more riding skill than trail riding, though that varies. Simply going along for the ride is not challenging, but when the weather is hot and dusty and cattle get contrary, things can become pretty intense. Driven by flies, hunger, or the desire for a greener pasture, cows can sulk in the coulee bottoms. Bulls can get mean. Although today's bulls rarely actually attack, their power is immense, and it is common for two of them to fight viciously, shoving each other all over in a cloud of dust, with total disregard for fences, people, or anything else that might block the way.

When Rockytop Tennessee, my faithful Walker gelding, was my *only* horse, my number-one hand in keeping up with the ranch work, we tangled with a Charlois bull in a one-on-one running battle that took up most of a morning. The bull, which belonged to my neighbor, was discovered peacefully grazing in my hayfield, a very antisocial activity, since the hay was nearly ready to cut and he was tramping it down. I called my neighbor (according to western tradition, it was his responsibility to retrieve his animal), who came down quickly. Knowing the man was horseless, I had already caught Rockytop, saddled him, and headed out toward the bull, hoping for an easy trip to the corral so my neighbor could truck him home.

The bull *looked* innocent enough, his white hide contrasting with the deep green of the irrigated timothy hay. Rockytop saw him and snorted. The young gelding did not like white cattle, felt they were something irregular, maybe even from outer space. He had already been unpleasantly surprised by a group of white cows, again my neighbor's, which had invaded our pasture and bedded down under a tree in tall grass. So surprised had Rockytop been when they flew out from under the tree, that he still, now at age fourteen, shies sideways a step and shows the whites of his eyes when we pass that tree.

But on this particular day Rockytop eyed the bull with cautious courage, apparently knowing he had a challenge ahead. At first the white bull herded easily enough. Then he got stubborn, then mad. The first time he ran up the fence line I tried to head him off with Rockytop, only to have him strike us smartly near the cinch on Rockytop's flank, knocking us sideways a couple of feet. (Thank God he had no horns.) Rockytop whirled and let go with both feet, rat-tat on the bull's skull, turning him. Then it was down the fence line in the opposite direction, this time the bull turning so quickly in front of us that Rockytop's chest slammed into the bull's side, knocking him down. But he was on his feet quick as a cat. Then the

*Crossing the big open. Photo: American Wilderness Experience.*

same scenario repeated itself: We would chase the bull, then the bull would chase us until Rockytop gave him both hind shoes, then we would chase again. After several of these engagements, the bull looked for an instant at the barbed wire fence, then charged it like a tank smashing through a chicken coop, accompanied by a chorus of wire squeaking through the staples and splintering fence posts.

My neighbor and my son then tried to turn the bull on foot at the head of the lane down which he ran like a white comet. If the bull noticed them at all I couldn't tell; they dived out of his way like scared chickens in opposite directions, and the bull disintegrated the gate they were trying to protect, Rockytop and I in hot pursuit.

Well, this was war. We rode hard to get between the bull and the highway and managed to turn him through still another fence, then flew down the lane in the opposite direction, toward the hills. The foot troops had dropped out by this time, and I found myself caring little whether my neighbor ever got this outlaw back. I just wanted him off the place. The head-to-head running duel continued, chasing until the bull turned to fight, exchanging blows, getting him running again, slacking off in hopes he'd settle down, the match continuing round after round with no sign of the bell. Our only encouragement was that he was headed east toward land that was my neighbor's. If he smashed just the right fences and crossed two more hayfields, we might land him in the neighbor's hill range.

And that is exactly what happened. By the time it was over Rockytop was covered in lather, I in water and mud from several flying trips across the creek, and the bull was slobbering from exertion. But there he was, across another destroyed fence, in my neighbor's hill pasture, heading up and out, his white, disappearing rear end the best side of him I had seen all morning. "Thank God and Greyhound…." We fixed fences all that afternoon and part of the next day. I have met a few individuals who can work cattle without ever cussing, but they are rare.

I suppose if there is a moral it is only to remember that cattle, like horses, are big, strong animals. If you have never worked with them their body language will be meaningless, but understanding will come with time. Leave any really sticky situations to the people being paid to handle them.

The enjoyable movie *City Slickers* did much to kick up an already popular horseback adventure, that of booking passage, so to speak, on a cattle drive, of really participating in moving the cattle. I would have some strong preferences, were I to choose this activity. I would ask whether the tasks were *real*, or simply created for guests. Some outfitters have two terminal locations and own cattle expressly to drive. One group of paying guests takes the animals from Ranch A to Ranch B, the next group from B to A and so on. I would have trouble enjoying such an artificial situation, though it might not bother some. Far better would be a cattle drive that was necessary for reasons other than satisfying guests. Many ranches offer participation on their twice-annual move from summer to winter pasture, for instance.

A ranch in Kimball, Nebraska, named 7 Springs offers a couple of events that fall into this "organic" category. Their fall roundup in October is a cooperative effort with several other ranches to gather cattle from summer pastures in preparation for the winter trail drive. Participating allows not only the opportunity to work cattle but also to "relive history from the back of your horse as you ride by abandoned homesteads and watch for teepee rings and Indian artifacts." There is also wildlife to see, from jackrabbits to mule deer. The 7 Springs brochure makes this cattle drive sound relatively recreational, with much emphasis on the barbecues and the camaraderie.

More suited to experienced riders, ones relishing some challenge and even discomfort, is 7 Springs's "True Grit Cattle Drive," a sixty-mile affair in November. This drive takes six hundred to seven hundred head of cattle from the ranch to their winter pasture north of Weldona, Colorado. Riding time is six to ten hours per day, and the words of the hosts reflect the demand today for rough-edged, challenging experiences: "We'll be screening applicants for riding experience and hardiness; this is not for the faint-hearted! We suggest you wear layers of warm clothing because the weather can get NASTY. Be prepared! This isn't an easy drive, but it's the REAL THING, and can be very rewarding."

As a professional cattleman I am initially amazed that people *pay* to have their feet numb with cold in the stirrups, that they look for chances to breathe dust, that they consider it a privilege to hear cattle bawling and see them milling at night in their mind's eye and ear. Then I stop to think how readily I abandon more necessary ranch tasks when it is time to saddle up and move cows around, how good I feel when it is accomplished. And I also realize readers of 7 Springs's advertising are looking for the new, the novel, for expansion of a life that has become too mundane. The cattleman we met in Spain, who we accompanied up a mountain, might have wondered why we would pay airfares and a healthy fee to do, basically, what we can do for free near home—ride horseback in the mountains. And yet we never questioned our actions, and we would go back in a minute. It would only be work if you *had* to do it. So I do not doubt that 7 Springs has plenty of applicants for its "True Grit" drive.

Another company offering an extensive schedule of cattle-related activities is The Cowhand Cattle Drives of Woodland Park, Colorado. Starting with branding in May, their schedule includes several cattle drives and culminates in a ranch rodeo during September. Their advance information contains a booklet entitled, "Howdy, City Folks," with information on branding, ropes, saddles, horses, and clothing. The orientation seems to be that of duplicating authentic cowboy experiences with a dash of in-town recreation along the way.

There are many others, of course, as the appendix shows. All, I am sure, will offer a microcosm of the Andy Adams experience. When the dust settles and the job is done, the hardships will mellow in our memories. Left in the center will be the accomplishment of doing a big job on horseback, a job impossible to do *without* horses. Whether it is the recollection of Rockytop's speed and courage in our running battle with the white bull, or the performance of all four of our ranch geldings more recently when we gathered our small herd from their eastern hill pasture and took them across the river, it is that partnership with our mounts that we remember with affection.

After many months on the trail, when they had reached the Blackfeet Agency, Adams felt that twist in the gut that accompanies the end of even difficult experiences:

> Another day's travel brought us to within a mile of the railroad terminus; but it also brought us to one of the hardest experiences of our trip, for each of us knew, as we unsaddled our horses, that we were doing it for the last time. Although we were in the best of spirits over the successful conclusion of the drive; although we were glad to be free from herd duty and looked forward eagerly to the journey home, there was still a feeling of regret in our hearts which we could not dispel. In the days of my boyhood I have shed tears when a favorite horse was sold from our little ranch on the San Antonio, and have frequently witnessed Mexican children unable to hide their grief when need of bread had compelled the sale of some favorite horse to a passing drover. But at no time in my life, before or since, have I felt so keenly the parting between man and horse as I did that September in Montana. For on the trail an affection springs up between a man and his mount which is almost human.

Adams goes on to describe the hardships man and horse shared over a drive of nearly three thousand miles, the rivers they swam, the stampedes they stopped, the long nights, and the dry trails, the horse "ever faithful, ever willing." He ends with a tribute to the horses in the remuda: "Their bones may be bleaching in some coulee by now, but the men who knew them then can never forget them or the part they played in the long drive."

*Chapter 6*

# Packing In

Many years ago I trudged up a winding mountain trail with another boy, his father, and my father. Dad and I had been invited to a fishing camp owned by the other family, a camp by Mystic Lake in Montana, accessible only by trail. There is a power plant at the lake, and a tramway owned by the electric company used to creep up tracks clinging to the side of the valley wall, but it did not take passengers. For a small fee, however, the company would consent to use the tram to transport fishing boats to the lake, so several nice semipermanent fishing camps existed there, and for me, at age twelve, hiking up the mountain to one of them was pure ice cream.

The climb to the lake was only three miles, but it was fairly steep, and my legs were better conditioned to bicycling than to hiking. Finally we gained the last high ground and were rewarded by a view of the lake, a blue gem two miles long, named Mystic because of its depth, which had been much exaggerated in those years with stories of futile attempts to find its bottom. We moved a short distance off the trail to eat candy bars and drink from canteens, enjoying the view, in no hurry to descend. From our vantage point Sigurd, my friend's dad, could see the locked storage container, made of a fifty-five-gallon drum, that contained his outboard motor and other valuables, his fishing boat beached securely alongside, and all looked okay.

While munching our snacks I heard the sound of iron shoes on rock, then looked up to see a slim, mustached man riding a sorrel horse. Soon the rest of the outfit came in sight, mules, a string of them, seven or eight if I recall correctly, all carrying packs. The man nodded "hello" to us but did not stop. I watched with growing fascination as the pack train left our trail and turned to the east, up the side of the steep mountain, where a trail, becoming in the distance as thin as a pencil line, switchbacked its way to the top of the valley wall. At that age I had no idea what lay up there. Now I know there is a high plateau with several mountain lakes good for fishing, and if one goes far enough, another valley with another river and chain of lakes. For me at the time it was like watching a ship go to sea until its hull dropped below the horizon, its destination unknown.

I was too young and ignorant of packing to appreciate some of what I was seeing. The man must have been an expert. It takes supreme confidence to lead a long pack train up a trail like that one alone. If you have a companion riding trail (the rear position) and something goes wrong with the pack of the fourth mule, fixing things is much easier. If a packer working alone must pass another pack train or turn his own completely around, his horsemanship had better be first rate. Even more important, his packing ability must be outstanding in the first place, because packing skills of high quality are necessary to avoid most of the wrecks likely to occur when one is alone. Packs so skillfully constructed that not a single adjustment need be made on the trail, even if an animal spooks or rubs against trees, are the packer's ideal.

Although impressed by the animals, I loved horses so much as a boy that I was not very discriminating. They almost all looked good, and as a town boy, the minister's kid, I would do nearly anything to finagle my way onto just about any equine with four legs. But a picture I can appreciate now hangs in my mind. The mules were all bays, all identical to my eye in size and build. Maybe I would not have understood the packer's pride at that time, but I do now. It was not enough that his mules be serviceable and sound; he wanted them to look classy, uniform in size and type. With neatly built packs on all the animals, he rode erect in the saddle, a mule man who knew what he was doing and took pride in it.

*Not all packers are men. Wanda Wilcox of Paintbrush Trails packs in guests, trail materials for the U.S. Forest Service, and hunters in the fall.*

But even at that age I had no trouble feeling an incredible attraction to what this man was doing. He was as self-sufficient as a human being can be in the wilderness. Not only was he prepared to take care of himself, he was equipped to set up a comfortable, even lavish camp for others far from the roads and trappings of civilization. I know now that he was probably establishing a fishing camp at a high lake for paying guests he would shuttle in later. As a boy, I did not care about the details. I only wished there was some way I could go along. Luckily, I was also quite boat crazy at this time, so I was not perturbed when Sigurd stood up and donned his pack, the signal we should move down to the beach. But I watched the packer until he cleared the crest and passed out of sight.

The picture I've related stayed in the back of my mind through years of growing interest in horses and packing, through the era when I considered packing mysterious enough to approach voodoo, then during the time I had learned enough to pack modestly with an animal or two and the simplest methods. Today I am not an accomplished packer in the professional sense, but give me a pile of gear, good animals, manty tarps, and Decker saddles, and I will get the stuff from point A to point B safely, in neat packs that do not come undone. And I will do so without injury to the stock. But regarding the packer's art, growing familiarity has not bred contempt, nor has the appeal been lost. Today I would watch that packer from years ago with an equal admiration for his skills and an equal tug in my heart to saddle up and be gone to the high country.

The pack train, like the sailing yacht, the snowshoe, and the dog team, is a primitive thing in its way. We have invented plenty of ways to go faster and farther, with more cargo aboard. But we have not come up with a more satisfying and efficient way to transport a comfortable camp into roadless backcountry, especially in areas where motorized vehicles are not legal or aesthetically pleasing. Little wonder that pack trips are more popular than ever, that small companies making pack saddles, wall tents, tent stoves, hobbles, and the like are doing bumper business. Twenty years ago in Montana I would have said the ranching and livestock business accounted for the greatest percentage of horse use in the state. Now I'm not so certain. A great number of Montanans own their horses exclusively because of their love for riding in the mountains, for summer pack trips and fall hunting trips.

To the person looking for horse-related recreation, the pack trip has great appeal, perhaps because such a trip can combine so many things. Often the pack trip is in conjunction with fishing or hunting. Sometimes the travel itself is the joy, and pack trains go long distances, setting up a new camp every couple of nights. Pack trips are also the ideal way to set up a base camp for lighter forays, perhaps on foot. They attract the same interest backpacking does, with the major differences that come with addition of horsepower. Pack trains can take heavier and more elaborate camping equipment. A woodburning stove in one's tent would be a prohibited luxury when all equipment had to be packed into the mountains on a packframe carried by a human. But it's commonplace in horse camps, as are cots, large tents with stand-up headroom, and Dutch ovens. (Those who have never sampled camp cooking by a Dutch oven connoisseur probably have no idea why anyone would want to pack such a heavy, ungainly item into a camp.)

Of course with today's needed emphasis on low-impact camping, on backcountry use that leaves little or no trace, heavy camp equipment is being discouraged. Using lighter camp equipment, the packer can take a party into the wilderness with fewer animals for less disturbance of the environment. Most horse packers have adjusted quite readily to practices that minimize the impact of large animals. Most use highlines to restrain their stock, avoid tying horses to trees because of the damage caused by pawing, pack in weedfree hay and pellets, and scatter their animals' manure when it is time to break camp. All garbage now is carried out, not buried, and campfires ringed by rocks are taboo. Instead, a shallow pit is dug, the ashes scattered, and the original sod returned when the camp is left.

Although some readers may eventually want to become packers themselves, owning the stock and gear necessary to be their own outfitters, that goal is only realistic for those who can keep their own horses and do so relatively close to their backcountry destinations. Self-outfitted pack trips are quite common in states such as Montana, Wyoming, Colorado, and Idaho. Ranchers, especially, must keep several horses year-round for their work and, as a fortunate sideline, have them available for recreation. But urban dwellers or those some distance from the backcountry they seek will probably be paying guests on their first pack trips. They will have the luxury of a professional packer to get the gear on the animals in such a way that it stays there and is carried humanely. Watching a professional, incidentally, is also the very best way to begin learning the necessary skills to pack on your own, if that is your aim. And even if you are paying a professional to pack you in, knowing a bit about the skills involved will take some of the mystery out of what the packer is doing when he or she is getting the animals loaded for the trail.

To get a better idea of the level of skill involved, consider the shape of nearly everything designed to carry cargo—a wheelbarrow, a pickup truck, the hold of a ship, or a shopping cart. All are boxlike, and all have a hollow holding area with sides. Then consider the back of a horse or a mule.

Nothing could be more opposite. Now getting miscellaneous stuff to ride securely on the back of the critter even though it moves, jumps ditches, bangs into trees, and spooks at everything that surprises it, is an art. And for both humane and practical reasons (an animal sored is useless the next day), the cargo must be carried in a way that does not chafe or hurt the pack animal.

Since human beings have been packing animals for many centuries now, approaches to the problem of keeping assorted items aboard four-legged critters have evolved to the level of art in many parts of the world. In the American West you are likely to see two types of pack saddles, the Decker and the sawbuck. The sawbuck, also called a crossbuck, is by far the older of the two. Versions of it exist all over the world. Looking much like a rack used for sawing firewood, for which it is named, the sawbuck consists of two pairs of wooden X's, the bottom legs of each X longer than the top ones. These X's straddle the animal's back, and between them, on the bottom legs, are two pieces of wood running front to back. These are the bars of the pack saddle tree, and they are somewhat contoured to fit the animal's shape. In the West sawbuck saddles are normally rigged with two cinches and, like all pack saddles, have a breastcollar and breeching. The breeching (often pronounced "britchin'" out West) keeps the pack saddle from slipping forward while the animal goes downhill. The breastcollar keeps it from sliding backward when ascending, just as it does on a riding saddle.

Usually the sawbuck saddle is used with panniers (often pronounced "panyards" in the West), bags, boxes, or baskets that fit on each side of the animal. These hang by short, looped straps or ropes from the sawbucks. I do not know how long panniers have been used, but there is reference to them in Shakespeare's plays, and I am certain they are far older than that. We saw huge, beautiful basket panniers in Spain, used to carry produce from vegetable farms to markets and restaurants. We also saw a type of pack saddle that had no tree at all but consisted of an extremely thick pad, made of two layers of cloth with stuffing of rye straw between them. These saddles seemed ideally suited for packing huge bundles of harvested grain, the main use we saw in southern Spain. I suspect they would not work for packing the hard, unyielding items often transported in the United States, from fuel cans to bridge planks to quarters of wild game such as elk and moose. We were told the Spaniards also use a saddle of the sawbuck type when similar cargo is to be packed.

*The Decker pack saddle, left, and the sawbuck, right.*

*A horse packed with a sawbuck, panniers, and a top pack, in this case secured by basket hitches rather than a diamond hitch.*

*A typical trailhead.*

In America today one is most likely to see panniers made of canvas or nylon cloth, or hard ones made of plastic. Traditionally, after he had loaded on the animal two panniers as close to the same weight as possible, the packer topped his sawbuck load with a top pack over the saddle and panniers. Then he secured a canvas cover over the top pack, using one of the many versions of the famous diamond hitch. The diamond hitch is an elaborate knot or lacing, which, when the hitching is complete, is diamond-shaped at the top. Tying a diamond hitch well was considered by some the mark of a first-rate packer, but that was probably not completely accurate, for those who used Decker saddles had no need for the diamond hitch, as I will explain. In any case, technology has moved in by providing top packs that secure cleverly with straps and need neither a tarp nor the security of the diamond hitch, a change mourned by some traditionalists.

Advantages of the sawbuck pack saddle include economy and adaptability to quite a variety of backs, assuming some skill with a wood rasp, for the bars can be whittled to fit. Several versions exist, including shorter ones for donkeys and llamas. A sawbuck saddle and a pair of panniers represent the easiest way for the novice to get started.

The Decker pack saddle was a product of the mining regions of Idaho, where an extremely rugged saddle was needed to pack bags of ore. The saddle looks like a large square saddle blanket with two iron D-rings protruding from the top. Actually, like the sawbuck, the Decker has two

*...ing a wild one. Photo: American Wilderness Experience.*

*A team of Belgians does its work on a wagon train in Montana.*

*Giving a packhorse some TLC.*

OVERLEAF: *An ancient threshing ring in southern Spain.*

Insert top: *We led our horses through most of the steep, slick streets of the villages. This street is in Trevélez.*

Bottom: *Spanish cattlemen run cows in the high country, just as some do in the United States.*

*Riding after an early snow.*

*An old mare on a pack trip makes a fine nanny for a young rider.*

*A couple heading out on a packing adventure beneath the Beartooth Mountains in Montana.*

*The author checks out Sugar's packs.*

*A mare packed with a Decker saddle and manties.*

wooden bars, but they are connected by these large iron rings. With a torch and some steelworking skill, one can adjust these saddles to the build of the pack animal, making them narrower or wider as needed. The blanket part is sometimes called a half-breed, and its function is to protect the animal's back and hold two wooden boards, one on each side, that distribute the load. The half-breed itself is stuffed with horsehair or other padding. A new version made of thick synthetic material is now available.

Although Deckers can be packed with panniers, a method called "mantying" is now generally preferred, and its advantages are many. A "manty" is simply a skillfully tied bundle made with a canvas tarp, secured with a series of half-hitches, then tied to the pack saddle, usually with a basket hitch. Although building a manty may seem difficult at first, the process is readily learned. Anything from bales of hay to bedrolls, bags of feed, sheepherder stoves—nearly anything of a size within reason can be mantied. Thus packing with manties is more versatile than with panniers, and once the packer becomes skilled at mantying he can have the camp on the trail virtually as fast. No supplemental covers are needed for the packs, for manty tarps are reasonably watertight. If they have any disadvantage it is that items inside manties are difficult to get at until the whole bundle is unpacked.

There are several concerns common to all packing. First, as mentioned, is balance. Panniers should weigh within a pound or two of each other, and it is far better to add a small rock to the lighter side than to tolerate imbalance. Manties can be a little less precisely balanced, for the heavier can be slung a bit higher than the other. This brings it closer to the center of gravity and thus in balance. The good packer is constantly looking back at the D-rings of the Decker or the sawbucks of the other type of saddle to make certain they stay centered on the pack animal's back. If they do not, he stops immediately and corrects the problem.

Another concern is the prevention of chafe or sores caused by improper padding. Panniers are packed with soft items inside against the horse, harder and more irregular items outside. Manties should be adequately padded by the half-breed, with its boards outside the padding to distribute the load. Good packers are constantly checking for anything that might rub and sore the horse. A good thick saddle pad fits under both types of saddles, and often it is larger than that used under a riding saddle.

It is important to remember that a pack animal is carrying dead weight. All but the poorest horseback riders help the horse by leaning forward while going uphill, backward while going downhill, and by moving cooperatively with the rhythm of the animal's gait. A pack does none of this. It is quite possibly as tough work for a pack animal to carry 150 pounds as for a ridden animal to carry 250.

Safety is a major concern as well. I mentioned the skills involved in leading a large pack train up a switchback trail alone. Good packers connect their pack animals together with several methods, but those used in the Rocky Mountains always include a breakaway link, often just a loop of baling twine, between each pair of animals. The idea is to prevent a large catastrophe, such as an animal going over the edge, from becoming a

*The author and family on one of their annual pack trips.*

giant one by its pulling the remainder of the animals with it. It takes nerves of steel to cope with a packstring when lightning starts crackling, snow begins to fly, or a grizzly bear contests the trail.

Now that we have some understanding of what is involved and some appreciation for the skills, let's assemble at a trailhead in the Rocky Mountains. You have booked a competent outfitter to take you into a wilderness area for a combination photography and fishing trip. You know, incidentally, that Curley is competent. He is licensed and bonded and has a good reputation. You have talked to others who have used his services, and all had fine things to say.

The trailhead has a parking lot, a small corral, and a chute for unloading stock trucks. Many pickups and horse trailers are parked in the lot, and you express concern that the wilderness is so well used. "Yeah, we'll see some people," Curley says, "lots more than when I was a boy. But there's a lot of country up there." He nods up the valley as he says that, and a breeze with just a touch of morning bite carries the scent of pine

*One makes all sorts of friends on pack trips. Photo: American Wilderness Experience.*

into your face. Looking up at the high, snow-capped peaks, you must agree. There *is* a lot of country up there.

This particular morning you will not learn much about building packs, for Curley is too well organized. He collected your sleeping bag and duffel last night, and while you shook off the jet lag in his rustic ranch kitchen he excused himself and disappeared. Now you know that Curley went out to the barn and assembled his packs. The manties are all made, ready to hitch onto the mules. The front animal will be packed with panniers containing items that may be needed on short notice, for they are easier to get at than if mantied. You appreciate Curley for his organization when you eyeball the packer readying another party across the parking lot. He is sweating over a huge bundle of gear, trying to organize and pack it. Curley will have you on the trail long before that packer gets mantied.

Curley seems to read your thoughts. "I like to get on the trail quick the first morning. But if you want to learn to manty, I'll teach you tomorrow." Then he asks you to bring over Cookie, a big bay mule so named, you learn, because she once stole dessert off a stump where the cook had set it to cool. "Don't walk behind her, even if you do it right with your hand on

*Packing in the Southwest. Photo: American Wilderness Experience.*

her rump and talkin' to her. She was handy with her heels just once, five years ago, and I've never trusted her since." You lead Cookie over as Curley readies a manty by standing it on end, his hands on the ropes, ready to lift. "How much does that weigh?" you ask. Curley tells you it weighs exactly eighty-six pounds—he knows because he weighed it back home. The matching manty weighs eighty-eight pounds, and he will equalize them by thrusting his ax through the ropes of the lighter one.

As Curley gets ready to hoist the manty in place, you feel a moment of conscience. He is no larger than you are, and all you are doing is holding the lead rope. "Can I—" you start, and he says "no" abruptly, even curtly. He lifts the manty smoothly, leaning it up against the mule's side, its bottom resting for a moment on Curley's stomach so his hands are free to bring a loop of rope up over the manty to cross it in front, then a free end from below which he pulls very hard, finally bringing it up to the crossing rope in front and tying it off. (You will learn later that he has tied a basket hitch.) Curley continues to exert some upward pressure on the manty, for there is nothing yet on the other side of the mule to counterbalance it. "It's the one place where a little beer belly doesn't hurt a guy," he says.

91

"Didn't mean to be impolite, but until you learn what I'm doing it's more trouble if you try to help. Now you can help me by lifting up just a little on this manty while I put up the other one. Don't feel you have to lift the whole thing. Just push up enough to keep the saddle from slipping over." Soon the other manty is in place, and Curley has you lead the mule out in a little circle, watching her critically. "Yeah, they look okay," he says.

The process is quickly repeated for each animal. Even though your job is a minor one, you are glad to be helping. You look across the parking lot at the other party, and you notice the couple are not interacting with the packer at all, are standing aloof in new and expensive-looking trail clothing. They appear to have met the packer here at the trailhead and seem to have given him a pile of gear he had not expected—he is shaking his head as he contemplates a guitar case—and you suddenly have more sympathy for his situation. For what you are paying Curley to take you into the wilderness, you certainly would have a right *not* to help him. But you are not going on a pack trip to be waited upon. You are going for a hands-on wilderness experience, and you find yourself asking Curley if there is anything more you can do. "No, as long as you've got all your personals in those saddle bags we tied on, just get on your horse and enjoy yourself. I'll put you in the rear so you can stop and take pictures anytime you want. The sorrel you're riding isn't hot stuff, but he's laid back enough he won't get hyper if the string pulls away from you."

You check the cinch on the sorrel, then swing into the saddle. As you follow the last pack mule in Curley's string, you cast one more clandestine glance in the direction of the other party. The man and woman are talking quietly, long looks on their faces, and the packer, his shirt sweat-stained, is cussing under his breath. He has things nearly packed, but the guitar case sits off to the side. You are glad you are not going with *them*. You also realize it is a great luxury to be packing in initially with just Curley. He will be bringing in a couple more guests tomorrow, but you will learn more helping him take in the camp than you would if the party were larger. You pass a trail sign that says, "Attention Stockmen: Uphill users have right-of-way till noon. Downhill users have right-of-way after noon. Parties should be on the trail by 9:00 A.M." You appreciate Curley's methods all the more.

The mules and horses seem anxious for the trail, trotting for the first, easy section of it until Curley eases back to a walk. He hollers back, "I like

*A folding sheepherder's stove can make a tent snug.*

*Camaraderie around the fire.*

*Two of the author's horses hitched to a highline.*

to let them trot for just a little ways, cause it's a good test of whether the packs are okay. If they aren't, something will shake loose." But the mules are certainly packed well, for the D-rings on the Deckers have stayed exactly centered on top of their backs. Curley says little more, for he is about a hundred feet ahead at the front of the string and there is the noise of the hooves and the gurgle of the creek next to the trail. That is all right, though, for now you enjoy slipping into your thoughts and the charms of the mountains around you.

All your life you have dreamed of this. Already, it is worth the money and the vacation time. A squirrel chatters, and you spot him flitting up a tree trunk. First the trail is gentle, an avenue through closely spaced lodgepole pine, then it leaves the creek and begins to ascend first one direction, then abruptly angles from left back to right, for the switchbacks have begun. Periodically Curley looks to the rear to check the packs, and when the animals breathe a little too hard, he stops for a "blow." Your sorrel horse needs an occasional dig of the heels, but you don't mind because he is so cooperative with your photography. You dismount many times, letting the pack string leave you, grab your shot, then trot the sorrel to catch up. Occasionally you shoot pictures from the saddle, using a fast shutter speed to stop the inevitable movement.

You meet a party of backpackers and notice Curley greets them enthusiastically. He tells you later he does this partly out of genuine friendliness, partly to get them to speak. "There is something about a backpack that changes the shape of a person and makes a horse wonder what the creature is. If they talk to you the horse understands it's a human." Curley tells you also that some horse packers don't like backpackers and vice versa, but that such feelings are silly and also less common now. "Packers sometimes figure since they and their horses were there first the backpackers don't belong, and the backpackers think the horses and their manure ought to stay the hell out. But you don't hear that stuff much anymore, and most backpackers are glad to see you." People are understanding that they have to share the backcountry that is left in order to preserve it.

There is one section of the trail that tightens your stomach. Above the timberline the trail becomes a three-foot-wide shelf with a cliff above and a cliff below. You are not particularly afraid of heights, and the three-hundred-foot drop would not be intimidating were you on foot. But the additional height of the horse above the trail takes some getting used to. You have been told to be watchful, yes, but to trust the surefooted mountain horse, for he does not want to fall any more than you do. The sorrel walks along as if he were crossing a corral on flat land, and the mules do not seem to notice the drop either. Curley shouts back that he's glad you won't be meeting another string—you can see clear to the top of the switchbacks, and no one is in sight—and later, with a twinkle in his eye, he tells you a story.

"Once I was coming up that stretch of trail with an eastern society woman clear at the back of the string. She was nice enough, but she wouldn't listen. Anyway, along that cliff she really spooked and started screaming her head off. Now the last thing I could do was stop that long string along *that* stretch, so for a minute I didn't know what to do. Finally, I just played dumb, pretended she was just going on about the scenery—she was a long ways back behind me, you know, and I couldn't hear her very good—so I just shouted back, 'Yeah, ain't it beautiful, though.' She stopped screaming, and she was fine when we got to camp, so nothing was ever said."

Camp tonight is in a hollow on top of the high plateau, green with tundra grass, a few scrub trees at this elevation. There is a delicious chill mixed with the warmth of the sunshine, and you pull out the down vest you stuffed, on Curley's advice, into your saddlebags. It feels wonderful. On the lake you can see telltale rings where trout are surface feeding. They will take a fly later if you just learned enough in that adult-ed fly fishing class to choose the fly they want. Curley points to a flat spot a hundred yards above the lake. "We'll camp there," he says. Then, oddly, he rides off to the side fifty yards, leading the string. "We'll take the mules over one at a time and drop their packs in the camp area. That way manure won't get left in our camp. Course, when we leave we'll scatter it all out so we're leaving back fertilizer instead of a mess."

There is much work to do, and you pitch in wherever Curley seems to need a hand. You notice he looks at you with more knowledge and respect than he did when he picked you up at the airport. First Curley tends to the saddles and stock, using a deadfall log as a saddle rack and covering all the saddles with a tarp. Then he hobbles the pack animals and turns them loose to graze. "I'm glad grazing is still legal here—it sure saves me packing in a lot of feed." Curley pickets his saddle horse, however, and feeds him a ration of pellets. "Like the mountain men used to say, it's better to count ribs than tracks. I'd rather he got a little thinner tonight than have

*A good packer keeps the D-rings on the Decker centered on the back.*

to be looking for him in the morning!" When the stock is taken care of, two tents go up, one acting as the cook tent, where Curley sleeps, another as the sleeping tents for the guests. You will have it all to yourself tonight, before the other women arrive. Then, with camp pretty much made, Curley digs a firepit, laying the sod carefully aside to make the pit disappear later without a trace.

"I'll cook us up some steak and potatoes," Curley says. "It won't be as good chow as the cook will turn out tomorrow, but it'll get us by." This time, you can tell, he does not want help. He wants to serve up his guest a good meal, so you let him, and the steak, rolled in flour and spiced with sage, tastes like meat from a wonderful exotic land. "It's elk," Curley tells you.

*A comfortable camp.*

The sun goes down and the stars come out. They are spectacular, brilliant here in clear mountain air at nine thousand feet. You never see them like that in the city. You have forgotten. You drink a sundowner with Curley, but he talks little. "Well, ma'am, if you don't mind I'll hit the rack and leave you with the fire. In the morning I'll get up real early to ride down and pick up your girlfriends. I'll leave you breakfast. You might try that fly pole."

"That's fine, Curley, but I might sleep in. I thought I was in shape for riding, but I'll admit I can feel I've gone a few miles. Good night."

"Good night. And thanks for the help."

Curley disappears, but you sit there a half hour longer. As it grows darker the stars brighten even more. You go to your saddlebags and retrieve a sweater to go under the down vest. But soon it is time to let the fire burn down, to think of fishing and a good book tomorrow. As you slip into your sleeping bag you hear the coyotes howl. This is fine. You will do this again.

## Chapter 7

# Adventures Overseas

We were stopped on a pretty section of mountain trail where irrigation water ran past the horses' feet, then diverted off the trail to another field below. Dallas Love, our guide, was carrying on an animated conversation with the farmer, who stood by the trail in rubber irrigation boots. Dallas sat her dappled gray mare with an easy grace, and the farmer, equally at ease, leaned on his shovel. Their words, not audible, floated toward me, mixed with the babbling water. I would learn later the subject of their conversation was horses (I might have guessed), more specifically, a horse for sale, the pretty white one picketed in the farmer's yard a quarter mile back. He was gentle, she was assured, and liked to run. That part the farmer might have saved if he wanted to make a sale—Dallas, like all guides who sometimes must put inexperienced riders in the saddle, did not need horses overly anxious to run.

I welcomed the pause to rest and reflect while Dallas and the farmer finished their cigarettes. I was struck more by the similarities to situations I had known in Montana than I was by differences. We were in a rugged mountain valley similar to those I knew at home, though the vegetation was different and the farming extended to a higher altitude. The irrigation ditches were like the many I had spent hours in back home, structured to pick up snow water from the high country and bring it down to thirsty fields. Our horses, like horses everywhere, fought the flies as best they could. The farmer was engaged in a task I knew well, diverting water in directions it was needed and away from areas that were too wet, using gravity and fighting it at the same time. And it was only proper to stop and visit with the farmer a while, whether he had a horse to sell or not.

But I was not in Montana. The irrigation ditches I admired were not engineered by the first settlers a mere one hundred years ago, but by the Moors more than five hundred years ago, before Columbus made his famous voyage. The farmer was not speaking English with the rise and fall of a Norwegian accent, common during my boyhood, but a southern dialect of Spanish. The mountains were not my beloved Beartooths, in the Absaroka range of Montana, but the Alpujarras, in the Sierra Nevada range of Spain.

Emerson called travel a "fool's paradise" (though he indulged in an extensive European tour himself), and Keats gave us a ditty about the naughty boy who ran away to Scotland, but found:

> *That the ground*
> *Was as hard,*
> *That a yard*
> *Was as long,*
> *That a song*
> *Was as merry,*
> *That a cherry*
> *Was as red—*
> *That lead*
> *was as weighty,*
> *That fourscore*
> *Was as eighty,*
> *That a door*
> *Was as wooden*
> *As in England—*
> *So he stood in his shoes*
> *And he wondered . . .*

*Dallas Love leads Emily, Christy, and Dennis past an ancient chestnut tree.*

But with due respect for the wisdom of Emerson and Keats, I think they minimized an essential point. To discover for yourself that the farmer in Spain caresses his scarce irrigation water during drought time, as I have done; that horse sweat smells the same on the other side of the globe; that not all farriers clinch horseshoe nails as tightly as they should; that a cold *cerveza* tastes fine after a hot dusty ride in Trevélez, Spain, just as it does in Nye, Montana—these are not travel disappointments, but reminders of what is universal in all of human experience. And the connections intensify that discovery. The Andalusian mare Emily rode, Paciencia, represented different genetics than our Tennessee Walkers. Yet, since the Spanish introduced horses to North America, might not this little bay mare share genes with the wild horses that run in the Pryor Mountains, fifty miles east of my home?

And along with the universal things, there are those totally new. A character in *Lonesome Dove* comments that there is nothing finer than riding a good horse through new country. Amen, to that; and there was nothing

*The farmer who tried to sell us a horse.*

newer to a couple who had never set foot on the European continent than the mountains of southern Spain. So Emily and I, wanting the ultimate extension of that *Lonesome Dove* experience, had for years coveted the trips advertised by the several agencies specializing in overseas horseback treks (see the appendix). When dreams edged toward reality we chose the Spanish trip offered by Equitour, a company based in Dubois, Wyoming, which offers several dozen tours in locations as exotic as India, Tanzania, and Argentina.

I had corresponded with Equitour's founder, Bayard Fox, about the concept of his company, and he responded eloquently:

> *The purpose of Equitour is to provide a wide choice of rides in the world's most beautiful and interesting places. We are constantly monitoring the rides, trying to upgrade them and seeking new ones. We do this partly by taking the rides ourselves, but equally important is the feedback we get from our clients. . . .*

*The horse in question.*

*So, for whom are these rides intended? They are for those who care about horses and riding, who have a strong spirit of adventure and are not afraid of new and strange experiences. They are for those who do not shrink from the occasional dust of the trail, patter of rain in the face or ache of tired muscles.... They are for those who are tired of glass, concrete, and traffic and whose hearts leap with joy and exhilaration at the freedom of a thundering gallop.*

Mr. Fox went on to explain that their clients need not be Olympic riders. The rides are rated as to difficulty, and the horses are matched to their riders' abilities. But implicit in Equitour's concept is appeal to those who joy in riding, not to the terribly unfit, to the complete beginner, or to one who wants to simply sit on a plodding animal and watch the scenery go by.

The choice of Spain was an easy one for us. Emily teaches Spanish in our local high school, and I have a rudimentary knowledge of it. Further, Spain, through Hemingway, Orwell, and others, has always seemed my second home. Since we were already addicted to riding in mountain country, the Alpujarra ride seemed tailored to us.

Though we had nearly a year to plan and prepare, our lives are too hectic to be truly organized for *anything* we tackle. So June came, and my Spanish was still unreviewed and my camera gear was not completely assembled. The myriad tasks to be accomplished before I felt I could leave the ranch, even in the capable hands of my sons, swelled to occupy every minute of the long June days. So maybe the long flight—Billings, Denver, Washington, D.C., Madrid, and, finally, Granada, Spain—was a necessary buffer, a time for nerves to settle and anticipation to begin building again. A layover in Madrid lasting most of the day allowed a quick side trip to the Plaza Mayor, an introduction to pesetas (and, in the expensive tourist section, how quickly they can evaporate), hard white bread, noisy but exciting streets, and the necessity of some knowledge of Spanish in Spain. It is *not* one of those European nations where "everyone knows English anyway," and even if it were, so many fine things would be lost without a foundation in *español.*

Then, after one more flight, this one on Avianca, over mountains beautiful but dry, much of them covered with olive orchards, we touched down in the city of Granada. Granada! The name rolls off your tongue with the lilt of the famous song, hung with the armor of knights and Moors and the stones of the Alhambra. The airport was startlingly small, considering the size of the city, much smaller than the one in Billings, Montana. In Europe, of course, there are more travel options, and I suspect most who travel from Granada to Madrid go by train. The customs officials did not bother with us at all. Once in the lobby we looked for a representative, someone, we hoped, with a sign, and felt some anxiety at our failure to spot one. That problem was relieved in a half hour or so, about as long as it took to figure out the Spanish phone system and call Dallas Love.

No need, for a Nissan Patrol 4 x 4 pulled into the parking lot. Out came Kristy and Dennis, the couple from Colorado who would be our partners on the trail, and a breathless Spanish driver named Fernando, apologizing profusely, mostly in Spanish, for his lateness, caused by traffic jams in downtown Granada, where he picked up Dennis and Christy. We had no trouble believing the traffic had been at fault, because we soon learned Fernando's driving could not have been the problem. This guy could thread a Mack truck through a China shop at a hundred kilometers per hour and never crack a glass.

For fifteen years I commuted 120 miles per day through Montana winters over mountain roads, normally at high speed with a coffee cup in one hand. I've eased my pickup with loaded horse trailer down logging roads, inches from a cliff, over ice. But, Fernando, I can't hold a candle to you. I couldn't stay on the bumper of your Nissan with a Porsche. We hurtled up the mountain road toward our first village, Bubión, around curve after curve, through an occasional town where the street narrowed to single-car, honk-before-you-plunge width. Fernando made up his time, delivered us safely to the *hostal*, and left us in the care of Dallas Love.

Dallas Love is an individual. Upon first meeting her, you do not type her in any way. Age or nationality do not come to mind. What does is a sense of her uniqueness as a human being. Here is someone who rides her own trail, who stubbornly lives the way she wishes. How many people must have told her, somewhere along the way, that she could do something more conventional than living in Spain, keeping horses, and to justify keeping them, taking all sorts of people on guided trips through the Alpujarras?

We would learn that Dallas was raised in this part of Spain, her British parents stationed there as agricultural advisers, that except for sojourns in an English boarding school and on a cattle station in Australia, she has lived most of her life in these mountains. Her knowledge of the local culture is as fluent as her Spanish. This first evening she quietly proceeded to get us organized, checked into our rooms, oriented, and prepared for the next day. And, after a fine late-evening meal (the Spanish custom), jet-lagged, having been up the equivalent of a day and a half, we slept our first night in Spain.

· · ·

We slept. Oh, did we sleep! The leisurely morning we had hoped for, before departing for the stables at ten, had all but evaporated before we awakened. Since we tend to be light sleepers, we took our grogginess to be our only really tangible evidence of jet lag. But we were in Spain, after all, ready to ride, and after a traditional Spanish breakfast, coffee and toast, we met Dallas's sister Eve for the ride to the stables. Eve, married to a Spanish dentist, is a delight. She pointed out that her driving habits were considerably more sedate than Fernando's. We had already noticed.

Dallas Love's stable is built on the mountainside above the white village of Bubión. (All villages in this part of the world are white, and one soon realizes why—they are cool havens when the Mediterranean sun beats down.) The stable is stucco, built in a square surrounding a small court-yard. Several horses were already tied out. Dallas introduced us to them. Most were Andalusian or that breed crossed with Thoroughbred. In talking to us the evening before, Dallas had asked enough questions to do most of the matchmaking.

Kristy would ride a gentle sorrel mare named Dorada, whose heavy bones and ample feather spoke of work blood in her lineage, while Dennis would ride another sorrel, mostly Andalusian. Emily would ride Paciencia, which means "patience." Dallas quickly told Emily that the mare was named after the quality her rider needs, not one the horse possesses. A beautifully built bay, Paciencia is capable of nervous quirks, but nothing more serious. And, saddled for me, sizing me up, muscular, plain, a tiny bit Roman-nosed, was a bay gelding named Bruno. Bruno is of mixed Spanish working stock. Dallas's choice of Bruno for me was recognition of two things, the second one complimentary. The first was that I'm a big, pretty heavy guy, and Bruno is very strong. I had lost weight for this trip, but the last few pounds scheduled were stubborn and thus still with me. The second was that Bruno was inclined to be lazy if allowed to be, but responded well to someone who could ride and would discipline him. Bruno and I had scarcely met before the words of Francis Parkman, describing his horse Pontiac in *The Oregon Trail,* came to mind: "a good horse," he said, "though of plebeian lineage," strong, but inclined to be stubborn.

The saddles would require some getting used to for Emily and me. Westerners to a fault, virtually all our riding has been in old-type western saddles with high pommels, cantles, and horns. I own an English flat saddle but have ridden in it only rarely. Dallas's English cavalry saddles were a bit more supportive than my flat saddle, but they still seemed insecure to us at first, besides hitting our anatomy differently. No matter, for we

*Emily and Paciencia.*

adjusted to them rather quickly. More seriously, my stirrups were small for my size twelve boot, the right one wanting to grab me. Like most horsemen, I'm absolutely phobic about the idea of anything knotting me to the horse, but this too was quickly remedied. At the first rest stop, we measured stirrups and found that Kristy's were a tad wider. Dallas switched them, and I had a whole new lease on Bruno.

We rode that sunny morning up a dirt road from the village of Bubión, then branched onto a trail. Although this section of Spain had been suffering from a devastating drought, it was still beautiful. I was struck by the similarity to our American Southwest and realized, for the first time, why the Spanish took so readily to that part of the North American continent. There were cactus and a plant like our yucca, with long, sharp spines. Some of the grasses, too, were the same as those on our cattle range in Montana. On the other hand, wonderful things grew here that would not survive in our colder climate. There were olive trees galore, along with chestnuts and other hardwoods. We rode past a chestnut tree Dallas estimated to be seven hundred to eight hundred years old; only the mountains are that old in Montana! There was scrub oak brush like we had known in Southern California and an oak that stays perpetually green like the "live oak" of the American South.

Everywhere were tiny terraced fields irrigated by ditches built many centuries ago. Oats seemed a dominant crop, often to be cut by hand for hay (Dallas's horses eat oat hay), then packed away in bundles by mules. There was, I realized, nothing "backward" about this. Farming in such locations on such tiny fields with large equipment would be impossible, even if the cost could be justified. Here was a civilization that had used all the space available, for the soil and the water had been good, and as Dallas said, "Everything grows here." Sadly, the drought and changing economic conditions are now leaving many of the terraces unfarmed and dry.

Dallas has a wonderful sense of her guests' riding abilities and desires. She guided her Andalusian/Thoroughbred cross, a stately, dappled gray mare, at just the right pace, a mixture of walk, trot, and, occasionally, fast canter. The horses were hard-muscled, long-winded, and surefooted. Toward noon they picked their way to a tiny village housing a little cafe. We enjoyed a fine meal there while the horses rested in the shade. After we ate, Dallas took the horses the remaining bread, which they relished.

After lunch we began to climb, part of the time on trails, part on what Dallas calls "tracks," in Montana, dirt roads. As we ascended, the familiar

scent of pine came to us, a touch of home. Much of this area was refor-
ested with pine seedlings by the Spanish government some years ago.

Soon we crested a divide between two valleys, enjoying frequent can-
ters, and heard the sound of gunfire. The shots were explained when we
came up on a parked vehicle with several Spanish men and boys engaged
in another activity commonplace in our home area, target practicing at
tin cans set up against a dirt bank. To avoid spooking the horses, the men
stopped shooting when they heard us approach. After a brief chat and
another couple hundred yards of riding, we heard explosions again and
thought the men had resumed shooting until we realized these booms
were bigger ones and were coming from the valley below. It dawned on
Dallas that Trevélez, our destination, was in the midst of a festival, and
that we were hearing their fireworks.

What an unexpected bonus! Most villages have just one such festival
each year, to honor their patron saint, and we were lucky enough to come
upon one. As we crested the valley and looked down on the beautiful,
white village, the percussion from the fireworks intensified. The horses
did not seem to care. Our anticipation built, meanwhile, as we picked our
way down the rocky trail.

On the outskirts of Trevélez, in a stable owned by a cattleman of Dallas's
acquaintance, we unsaddled our horses and helped settle them in for the
evening. An orphan calf with bell darted in and out of the barn. Then we
started down the path toward the village. Dallas asked which we would
prefer, to stop by the place we would later be eating, where there was beer,
or to go to the hostel first, where there was no beer. The one-syllable
answer from everyone was "beer."

The bar/restaurant turned out to have the entire fiesta camped right in
front. A cheering crowd indicated some sort of contest, especially exciting
because it involved horses and mules. A clattering of hooves drew our
attention to a steep street descending from a small square. Several young
men on horseback were racing down the street and trying to snatch a
ribbon off a rope, then return to the top of the short street first, thus to
win and present the ribbon to the young lady of choice. Meanwhile, a line
of a half-dozen pretty girls, gorgeously arrayed in fiesta dresses, acted as
cheerleaders so vigorously my camera shutter speed could not freeze them.
We squeezed our way through the ecstatic crowd and into the bar while
the band, high-school-age musicians, struck up a lively march. So we sipped
San Miguel and watched and listened. Now *this* was Spain!

If I could afford to have a vacation home anywhere and the plane tickets to travel there regularly, a small home in Trevélez, Spain (with a stable and horse, of course), would be a top contender. I loved all three of the villages in which we stayed—Bubión, Trevélez, and Berchules—but it was Trevélez that held on to me. All three were white but bestrewn with flowers, color growing in pots everywhere, on every iron balcony railing. The streets in these villages are extremely steep; to walk to your neighbor's or to the store is enough for cardiovascular health. Dallas rues the day they covered the native stones, laid on edge by the Moors for great traction under hooves, with concrete for the convenience of bicycles, motorbikes (the bane of Spain), and automobiles small enough to squeeze into them. True, they grooved the concrete, but it is still slippery, and we always led our horses through the villages.

Each of the mountain villages also had at least one picturesque water trough for watering stock, fed by spring water through pipes. Before indoor plumbing these were used to slake human thirst as well. Even now, villagers fill water jugs at some of them. Dallas knew the water quality in each and kept us posted.

Everywhere in these villages, even when there is no fiesta, people are out walking, and in the evening before late dinner the whole village spills onto the streets to visit, to walk, or to sit in the shade. People were universally friendly to us. Their Andalusian mountain dialect tested our limited language ability. Emily's Spanish was unhesitatingly understood, but their answers to our questions came rapidly with dropped syllables and words combined. *Buenas noches* became *buen noshe* to my ear. Of course, we make similar changes in our own language, but the deviation from the Spanish we had learned was enough to throw us a curve.

Trevélez, my favorite village, was originally built in three sections, now merged enough to be less discernible. Dallas told us two legends of why this occurred. One was that a Moorish ruler had three sons, and he built a section for each. The other was that the three segments represented class divisions, a section each for the farmers, artisans, and businessmen.

She also explained a feature of the Spanish farm economy that dates from the Moors. Each villager had a farm, but in three separate sections, not one block. There was a garden plot near or in the village, a terraced field partway up the mountain, and a remote mountain pasture. The third, the "summer farm," a section of highland occupied by a family during summer for tending livestock and raising a small grain crop, exists even today. Later on the ride we would see many of the flat-roofed stone dwellings, some still in use, on such farms. But many today go unoccupied, and this productive custom will probably die.

On our first night in Trevélez (the second would be later in the week), when we returned to the cafe for our evening meal, a fog and slight drizzle had set in. No real rain resulted, but we thought the change in the weather might dampen the fiesta. We did not yet know the Spanish very well. This was the third and last day of the fiesta, Sunday (though Monday would be taken as a holiday to recover). Again, luck had it that the very culmination of the event would take place right in front of us. First, we watched a spirited piñata party, the piñata made of pottery, unlike the Mexican ones we know well, dangling from a rope, a stern referee hanging a new one each time a hit was scored. Then the parade, the same beautiful girls now carrying a platform on which rested the statue of San Antonio, emerged from a side street to the accompaniment of the band and the crowd.

They paused in front of the church door for a series of cheers to the health of the village, culminating in "Viva San Antonio!" It was a combination of soccer-level cheering with a reverence that reminded me this was, too, a religious event. Then all went into the church for a short mass. The event, more than the sudden chill in the weather, put goose bumps on my arms, and I retreated into the cafe for warmth and dinner.

We were too tired to be kept awake by the fiesta, even though music, cheering, and fireworks filled the air until at least four A.M. When I awakened it was always briefly, the exciting sounds a nice backdrop to sleep, not an interruption. And when I awoke for good the sun was up and the village, finally, was quiet.

• • •

On a busy schedule there is little time to reflect. That comes later, and now our equestrian adventure in Spain is a series of highlights indelibly sketched on my mind and Emily's. The chronology of the trip grows less important, the things with staying power more so.

The horse has had a powerful role in the history of Spain. Her culture is a medley of Andalusian steeds, Arab seed stock, the Spanish Riding School (exported to Austria), and the bullfight, with all its pageantry on horseback. In rural southern Spain, in crowded village settings, two fine houses will still flank a stable, a finely bred neck and head of a horse emerging over a Dutch door, the horse taking its air. Horses and mules are used, really used, for farms inaccessible to vehicles are still part of the economy.

Dallas told of us of the wonderful fairs in Sevilla and elsewhere centered around the horse, spring fairs we must return some day and see. She also conveyed fears that some of this equestrian tradition must inevitably disappear, just as it has in the United States, as need for the horse diminishes. Recreational uses keep the horse important, of course, but I suspect Dallas was thinking of the understanding that comes with horses when they are your everyday working partners. Dallas also explained that the bullfight is a catalyst for a host of horse-related traditions, training, and craftsmanship.

The mules in Spain are as enjoyable as the horses. We were told that until recently it was common to see extremely well-bred saddle mules, creations of the best mares when bred to Spanish jacks. I did see many with beautiful conformation, mules that would be greedily purchased today in the American West, where well-bred mules are becoming more popular. In addition to those doing daily work on the farms, we saw mules earning a living on the Costa del Sol, in sophisticated truck farming and hothouse operations, carrying produce to market and trenching crop rows for irrigation. And then there were the old mules, many thirty and even forty, picketed outside the villages, their masters aged, retired farmers who had been unable to part with them when they had moved to town.

To one who ranches in Montana, meeting Spanish cattlemen was another treat. It was the second day of riding, when we switchbacked up the mountain trail that took us high above Trevélez, that we met a slim, dark man on a white horse. His saddle was typically Spanish, with high backrest, equipped with a crupper, like ours, to keep the saddle in place when riding steeply down. He rode with the easy grace of those who spend much of their working lives in the saddle, guiding his horse with the single rein prevalent in Spain. (I assume the horse neck reins in one direction, direct reins in the other.) One arm was in a cast, and a cane was thrust through the saddle strings. We were to learn he had been leaning off the side of his horse in an awkward position when the animal elected to jump a ditch, that he had fallen and broken his arm in seven places. None of this was

*Rest stop by an ancient mill.*

keeping him from riding up the mountain to tend his stock, of course. I assumed the cane was there only because of the injury, but changed my mind later when we met his partner, uninjured, who also carried a cane.

We stopped to view pretty Trevélez, far below us now, while Dallas and the cattleman shared her cigarettes. We would accompany the cattleman some distance up the mountain, where he would locate his cows and join up with his partner, who was bringing cattle over from the next drainage. Then they would move the bunch to better pasture. The drought was forcing this adjustment a couple of months earlier than was normal.

Later, higher on the mountain, when the only real chill of the entire trip had forced us to don pullovers, we rested again and watched the second cattleman bring a group of cows and calves over the mountain. Assisted by three good cow dogs, he pushed them down the narrow mountain trail until he joined us. Then we parted company, but not for good. At our lunch stop, when Dallas had served us "picnic"—salad, sausage, bread, goat cheese—the two men showed up again, refusing food but enjoying a visit, their well-trained dogs staying out of the picnic circle but relishing scraps Dallas threw them. We learned the men were missing a calf and would proceed toward Berchules, the next village, to look for it.

*One of the many threshing grounds built by the Moors.*

Two days later, back in Trevélez, we encountered the first cattleman again, leading his horse through town, and he said they had found the calf.

The cattlemen were kindred spirits. They face the problems of cattlemen everywhere, worries about grass and water and drought. But there was pride in their faces as they sat their horses, an aura of independence and strength surrounding them. Like American cattlemen, they pay the government a fee for grazing the high country. Unlike their American counterparts, they do not seem to have faced forces that consider cattle "politically incorrect," which consider grazing inherently destructive (though bovines have grazed the ranges for thousands of years). Indeed, above one of the villages, at the end of a long day, we heard a cow below, and Dallas said, "There is always something comforting about hearing a cow moo in the valley."

The first of the cattlemen had been interested when Dallas said Emily and I were *vaqueros*, that we had cattle in far-off Montana. He wanted to know what kind mine were, but the term *Angus* meant nothing. Hearing I had black cows and red cows, all without horns, got his interest though,

114

*Author with Pacienca, left, and Bruno.*

and he asked how many we had. We are very small operators by Montana standards, running just eighty cows, but I could not tell if the Spaniard thought that was a large number or a small one.

There were other kindred spirits, too. The children of the villages liked horses, as all children do, and enjoyed seeing them pass, the smallest in the arms of adults who told them about *caballos.* Emily struck up a friendship with a band of kids in Berchules who played near our stable. The little boys were busy chasing the little girls in order to slime them with mortar from a nearby building project. But the oldest of the girls, a slim blond one (yes, there were blonds here, though in this area of Spain, with its Moorish past, most are dark) kept her poise. She got the boys back in line, then wanted to know Emily's name. *"Me llamo Emilia,"* Emily told her, whereupon the girl introduced the whole gang, sister, cousins, and the naughty boys. The next day the blond girl saw us again and greeted Emily by her name.

The land, too, was kindred. One who loves the American West must automatically love Andalusia, especially when he or she sees it from the back of a horse. Even near the large cities there is an openness like ours in Montana, a feeling of elbow room poles apart from the crowded, noisy city streets. The land, strapped as it was by drought, still seemed giving, productive, anxious to please. In the high mountain meadows thyme grew, several varieties of it, which Dallas picked and passed back, the tiny flowers smelling wild. Along with thyme there was rosemary, spices from the Simon and Garfunkel song that is a favorite of ours and our youngest son Steve. We had a fleeting desire to put samples of these in a Ziplock bag and take them to him when we returned, before we remembered customs and what they would suspect of herbage in a plastic bag.

Wherever water was adequate, things grew more than willingly. Lower in elevation there were raspberries and strawberries, peach and pear trees, and all the usual salad ingredients grew in beautifully tended gardens. There were cherry trees, one in particular that we all enjoyed. Its location was interesting, because it grew on the edge of a threshing ring. All over this section of Spain, even very high on the mountains, one encounters circular, level areas, rocked up on their lower sides and floored with flagstones. These range in size from about fifty feet across to several times as large. In mountains grain is grown on terraces, and when the grain is ready, a level place is required to thresh the grain. These threshing grounds provided that, along with a clean floor. Most were built by the Moors, though Dallas mentioned two even more ancient, built by the Romans.

We rested our horses on the threshing ground with the cherry tree and learned that Spanish horses know how to eat cherries right off the branches. We, too, ate our fill, probably too many, while Dallas had a conversation with the farmer who worked in his stable adjacent and who had said we could help ourselves. Dallas always visited with the people we met. She understands the culture, is truly part of it, and custom says you stop and visit. You don't just say "How are you?" without expecting an answer, as we do in urban areas (when we speak at all). When I was a boy the Norwegian ranchers were the same way. You did not stop by the homestead for business only, and you didn't fail to go in for coffee.

It was on the third day of riding, in the valley above Berchules, that we encountered the farmer who tried to sell Dallas his horse. That extremely rugged valley, with rock outcroppings, reminded me most of several drainages near our home. Yet it was also the one that spoke most strongly of antiquity. In addition to usable rock dwellings for summer farms, older ruins, many of them elaborate rock structures clinging to the mountainsides, were prevalent. We had a rest stop by the ruins of a stone

*Emily's friends in Berchules.*

mill by the stream. Never finished, according to Dallas; the Spaniards who repopulated the area in more recent times had been unable to figure a way to get water to it. Either the original designers had made an error, building it too high above the streambed, or they knew some sort of secret.

The temperature had risen, and horseflies were more common this day. These bothered the horses and also gave Dallas a tough time while she prepared our midday "picnic" in a grove of trees at the bottom of the valley. The trees were a type of poplar virtually identical to our Montana cottonwoods. But the picturesque little stream, clear and cold, was a mere shadow of the river it had been before the drought. Dallas kept pointing out the proper streambed, now high and dry. Yet, it was nearly perfect, and had I found this site in Montana, I would have pitched my wall tent, rigged a highline to picket the horses, and settled in.

As it was, in spite of the flies, we had another one of Dallas's fine picnics. She had brought the ingredients for a salad, so she first sliced vegetables into a big plastic bowl, then gave it her usual vinegar-and-olive-oil treatment, standard, it seems, in Spain. Again there was fresh white bread, the small, hard-shell loaves, sausage, ham, and white goat cheese bought from the shepherds.

The ham, especially, bears special comment. We were in a section of Spain famous for its hams. Everywhere in the villages are ham-curing houses, and new ones are under construction. Even these extensive, multistory buildings apparently do not provide enough space, for hams hang in every bar, restaurant, and *hostal* lobby, drip cups attached, lending their fragrance to the surroundings. (I did think the hams that hung in the bars had to be at least partially cured by cigarette smoke!) Upon our return we found even our home-town butcher in Montana knew about hams cured in the mountains of southern Spain.

I was, however, perplexed by the relative scarcity of hogs. Of all the barnyard animals, pigs of any kind were the most rare. There were many wild boars, we heard, creatures that readily cleaned up any food left behind at your picnic site, but few domestic ones. Dallas explained the apparent paradox. Once many hogs were raised here, and the area became famous for its cured hams. As it became less economical to raise them, the market for cured hams remained strong, even increased as this area became famous for the product, thus the butchered hogs were imported just for the curing process.

The ham that results from this cure is quite different from that eaten by Americans. Not even-textured and nearly mushy, Spanish ham is drier, stringier, and tastier. It is best sliced quite thin. Laid between two pieces of Spanish bread, topped with goat cheese and a bit of mustard, it is a feast.

The area is famous, too, for its trout, a creature hard hit lately by the drought's effect on the streams. Looking at the clear water and thinking of my fly rod back home, I could only wish for the return of the rain. I thought of that fine scene in *The Sun Also Rises*, in northern Spain, when Jake and his friend fish a sparkling stream, then have lunch with wine chilled in the creek.

Tourism, also, is a growing industry in this part of Spain. We met busloads of German and British tourists, some of whom had walked to the top of Mt. Veleta, 3,470 meters (11,384 feet), the planned site of "Sierra Nevada '95," the world alpine ski championships. All of Spain hopes for the snow to return—the T-shirts are already on sale! We saw Mt. Veleta's sister, Mt. Mulhacén (3,481 meters), the tallest mountain in Spain, from two different sides during the course of our ride.

*A narrow street in Granada.*

Given this aura of tourism, we were not surprised to meet a newspaper reporter from Granada who had traveled down to cover the festival in Trevélez. Dallas was buying groceries for the day's lunch while we held the horses, and the reporter knew quickly that Emily was the one most likely to understand him. They held a fine conversation. Curious about renting horses, the man was looking for Dallas. He ended up photographing us all horseback in the town square, disappointed we did not have time to join him for a glass of wine. It was ten A.M., but that poses no conflict in Spain.

One must live in a foreign country for many years before claiming to know the people. We cannot say that happened on our short stay, but we *can* say we liked what we saw and who we met. It seemed more than friendliness we encountered—perhaps naturalness is a better term. People did not perform for us in any way, even though we were often in places where Americans must be exceedingly rare. Oh, I did notice the officer of the *Guardia Civil,* the national police, on a balcony above the street, stand up and pull in his gut and look commanding when he saw three nice-looking ladies, Dallas, Emily, and Kristy, approach on horseback. But he was merely, as they used to say on *Candid Camera,* "caught in the act of being himself."

Part of the ease of relating to the people must have been the horses. Animals are a universal catalyst. At one of the *hostales* a shy woman altered personalities abruptly when I took interest in the parrot on the terrace. She rushed over and had him perform for me, had him say *hola,* whistle, and shake my finger. The effect of seeing visitors on horseback was even more profound, for the horse is linked to Spanish culture, to Spanish past, and tourists riding horses are not completely alien.

There were five days of riding in all, an average each day of perhaps fifteen to twenty miles. Our schedule was tailored to fit Spanish customs. We had a very light (coffee and toast) breakfast each day, began riding by ten or so, had lunch in a village or one of Dallas's picnics around three, then reached our destination about six. That allowed several hours to clean up in time for dinner at around nine P.M. We spent two nights in each village, the first and sixth in Bubión, the second and fifth in Trevélez, and the third and fourth in Berchules.

Berchules was the most agricultural and least "touristy" of the three. We found a bar with fine *tapas* there, the generous snacks served with each drink in this part of Spain. I am told an early king tried to raise an army from a populace that was protein-starved but among which wine flowed readily. He ordered that a substantial serving of meat be presented on top of each wine glass and that the food be consumed before the wine was. *Tapas* are free in this part of Spain, but they charge for them in the more metropolitan areas.

It was in Berchules, too, that we were introduced to telephones that greedily devoured one-hundred-peseta pieces. We'd neglected to record the magic number that accessed our phone company in the States, a mistake we'll not make again, for without it we could not call by credit card. (Later, on the coast, we found it published.) Still, we were able to contact our sons and get a ranch report, learning to talk fast while the pesetas held out.

Each of our five days of riding took us over new terrain, and we duplicated an earlier trail only once, for just a mile or so. That was on our second entry into Berchules, past the cherry tree, for a chance to repeat our treat. We've been asked whether five days was about right, and we think so. For one traveling all the way to Spain for the horseback experience only, fewer days in the saddle would seem expensive, since one's airfare would be as costly as for a longer trip. Further, we are all limited in how quickly we adjust to new experiences and situations. I'm not certain we would have settled into the aura of backcountry Spain, adjusted to the point of maximum appreciation, if our horseback experience had been shorter. The cost per person, by the way, in 1994 U.S. dollars, was approximately $1,000 at the time we took the trip. This included all food and lodging, plus a sixth night in a Granada hotel, except for drinks and incidentals. (Airfare is additional.) A pocketful of pesetas lasted a long time during the week with Dallas.

But the week in the mountains did go fast. Since we had other adventures to look forward to, that last night in Bubión, when Dallas, Kristy, Dennis, Emily, and I ate fine steaks and drank several toasts, did not mark the end of our Spanish experience. We would return to Granada and drive a rental car to the Costa del Sol, there to spend several fine days on the beach in one of the coast's quieter villages.

But socializing on the terrace under stars, looking at the village lights in the valley below, was very fine because of what we had done as a group. The shared experience on horseback was a bond, and Dallas Love was the catalyst. This was the last we would see of her on this trip (we're trying to talk her into coming to Montana to ride with us, and I think she is tempted).

The impression this independent woman left on Emily and me is very strong. In an age when many speak of independence, of equality between sexes, of doing one's own thing, Dallas actually lives that way. We will think of her long in all her roles, tossing the salad on our picnics, being firm but gentle with the horses. One moment she would say, "Tomorrow a stick for you, Bruno" and the next speak to him and the others with quiet affection. And her horses' response to her was always evident in ears cocked in her direction whenever she spoke. Dallas is totally herself. We will long carry the image of Dallas Love astride her stately, dappled gray mare.

And so we left to be tourists, to walk over the grounds of the Alhambra, poke into the shops on the narrow, noisy streets of Granada, bask in the sun, and test the water on the Costa del Sol. Spain for us will always be a medley of little delights, *tapas*, Fanta (the soft drink we adopted, in lemon), crusty bread, good local wine, the pudding called *flan*, and insatiable telephones. There were the pop machines that also held cans of *cerveza*, *insane-but-skilled drivers*, and *descafeinado* (decaffeinated coffee) for Emily, *café con leche* for me. (I finally found how to approximate American coffee, for black coffee in Spain is espresso. One orders *café negro con agua caliente*, or in the tourist areas, *café americano*. Then they bring you espresso with hot water on the side. When mixed you have, almost, the stuff to which I'm addicted.)

But more poignant still will be thyme growing on the mountainside, the cattlemen looking for their calf, the terraced fields, and the sounds of hoofs on the rocky trails and the village streets. There will be in my mind the farmers hurting for moisture, their situation prompting me to say to Emily, spontaneously, as we boarded the plane in Granada, "I hope it rains for them." And always, for us, Spain will be inseparable from the horses.

Would we go again? To Spain, for sure. On another foreign horseback adventure? Again, the answer is yes, but Equitour and its prime competitor FITS Equestrian, along with several smaller companies, offer such a smorgasbord of tantalizing possibilities, we would have the kid-in-the-candy-store problem if fortunate enough to go again. An African adventure would be wild, and Australia has always beckoned. On the other hand, we both know a little Norwegian, and those Icelandic ponies are gaited like our Walkers. Who knows? But we really do not expect future adventures to eclipse the views of the Alpujarras, the village of Trevélez, and Dallas's gentle "Canter on."

# Chapter 8

# The Endurance Trail

Pretty much absent from this book on adventures with horses has been the whole realm of competitive events. That is by design. Certainly many such events, from dressage to bronc riding, showing to roping, three-day-eventing to foxhunting, qualify as adventure with horses. But when I envisioned, earlier in this book, the Indian brave on his vision quest, I saw a vantage point from a high place, I saw earth and sky and distance. So western is my orientation, so influenced am I by my open, big-sky environment, that it never occurred to me to include in this book events that take place in arenas in front of grandstands and panels of judges.

I admire most such events greatly. Dressage is the epitome of the rider/horse relationship. The cowboy who climbs on a saddle bronc, repeatedly, even after broken bones and hospital stays, has guts, period. But I have never been fond of riding a horse in an arena. Emily and I raise show-quality Tennessee Walking Horses, and some of our customers do use them for show. When I hear of one of our colts finding success in the ring, I am proud. But those we keep for ourselves herd cattle and carry us and our packs into the mountains.

When I train a colt for myself I ride him several times in a small round corral, several more times in an arena, and then get him out to the hills, where the remainder of his training takes place. I admire the things one can teach in an arena, but I must confess that riding a horse in a corral for hours on end is too much like sailing a beautiful boat in a swimming pool. In each case you have something made to travel to other worlds, and confinement seems incongruous. The old-timers in Tennessee had a saying about a good horse. "He's always looking for the next town," they said. Our horses are always looking for the next mountain.

But there *is* a type of competition that attracts me, that I admire greatly, and that I may try myself some day. I am referring to the evolving sport of endurance riding. Endurance riding takes place in the great outdoors, often in beautiful terrain. Like packing in and riding a wagon train, endurance riding is linked to our past, though perhaps not to the most fortunate sides of it. An American Indian caught in the open by members of an enemy tribe was suddenly in an endurance situation. It was not enough that his horse had to run faster and longer than the *average* one chasing him. It had to run faster and longer than the *best* in the enemy group, and probably, usually, it did not.

A more enjoyable sort of endurance riding practiced by the Plains Indians was buffalo running. It was just that, running, for the buffalo killed were butchered by the big crowd of women and children following the chase. The hunter did not have to stop after he sank an arrow into a representative of the tribe's winter meat supply. That such occasions covered great distances was discovered by the historian Francis Parkman when he took part in a buffalo hunt on his horse Pontiac. He reported, in *The Oregon Trail*, that he was caught up in the chase and quite lost when it was over, for he estimated he was a good twelve miles from the starting point.

People out West practiced other types of endurance riding as well. Certainly one of the most famous was the Pony Express, in effect a relay race to transport the mail as rapidly as possible. Put out of business by the telegraph after a few short years, the Pony Express coupled light riders with ultralight saddles and horses that could run twenty miles flat out, the rider jumping onto another horse held waiting for him at each of the stations.

The Arabs, of course, were perhaps the world's masters when it came to traveling far and long, so it is no surprise that the breed they gave us is the dominant one used for endurance riding today. But before something done historically out of necessity is converted to a sport, we must look long and

*Our friend Cliff Knighton and his mule Opie. Cliff's explanation for being crazy enough to ride an endurance race bareback: It avoids saddle chafe!*

hard at the ethics involved. If someone were chasing you with intent to kill, being overly concerned with the welfare of your horse would simply result in your death. I think of Tolstoy's character in the story "The Prisoner of the Caucasus," chased headlong over rough terrain by Tartars on fine horses. I think of his affection for the game little mare he is riding, the regret for having to use her so harshly. But I doubt whether anyone could seriously expect him to put the life of the horse above his own in such a horrible, but historically realistic, situation.

But horse-related sports are a different story. Our lives do not depend on them, so to feel right about these activities we must carefully safeguard the health of our horses. To simply turn a group of riders loose on a fifty-mile race and offer a large prize to the first rider over the finish line would encourage all kinds of abuses. Endurance riding in the United States is not carried on that way at all. In fact, endurance riding has evolved as probably the equine sport *most* careful of all for the welfare of the horse. What other competition requires periodic checks of the animal by a veterinarian to see that it is in good shape to continue? How many equestrians in other sports carry stethoscopes to frequently monitor their horses' heartbeats or are sophisticated enough to tell by a pinch of the skin whether their animal is dehydrated? How many would know to be concerned if their horse stayed "inverted," that is, maintained a respiratory rate higher than its heart rate?

We were able to watch the sport recently in Roundup, Montana, on the three-day weekend of the Bull Mountain Ride. Our vantage point was the vet-check area, an ideal place to get a feel for the event. Our friends Cliff and Sue Knighton were heavily involved, Sue as the veterinarian in charge, Cliff participating as a rider on his mule Opie.

One immediately notices some differences between the crowd of horses and people at an endurance ride compared with those at other equestrian events. The people themselves look physically well-conditioned, most on the thin side, and so do the horses. A healthy endurance horse shows a little of his rib cage, is consistent with the old saying, "a lean horse for a long pull." A woman we know had to quit showing her stallion when she began endurance riding, for optimum conditioning for endurance made him appear too thin for the show ring. Dress is for function, not show. Some riders wear shorts, but most favor spandex pants, though some ride in loose-fitting jeans. Many wear riding helmets for safety, but these folks are an individualistic lot, so it is not surprising that some favor baseball caps, cowboy hats, or no headgear at all. (There are endurance events, however, that require helmets.) Footwear varies, some riders wearing traditional western or English boots, but others favoring running shoes, sometimes of the style with more heel, designed for riding. It is permissible to lead your horse, so footwear comfortable on the ground is important.

A quick look at the horses shows that Arabians are king in this sport. Many other breeds do well, with some Thoroughbreds, Morgans, Tennes-

*The vet check area is a busy place. Dr. Sue Knighton checks the hip of a mule.*

see Walking Horses, and Quarter Horses competitive, though heavily muscled Quarter Horses (or heavily muscled animals of *any* breed) are conspicuous by their absence. Muscles are wonderful, but too many of the wrong kind are impossible to fuel over endurance distances. These horses, remember, are the equivalent of human marathon runners. We learned that the Morab, a Morgan/Arabian cross, is quite popular, and several mules participated. All horses must be at least five years old, and few of that age are campaigned aggressively. Just as human marathon runners often do not peak until they approach middle age, the most competitive endurance horses are usually from around eight to twelve years of age, though many much older do well.

Two lengths of ride were occurring simultaneously at this particular event: twenty-five miles on two consecutive days and fifty miles on three consecutive days. The people in the twenty-five-mile race were the less serious about garnering points and victories. Only a best-conditioned award was given for these shorter races, and they presented an opportunity for riders to evaluate their horses for more extensive competition.

*Dr. Knighton during a rare lull.*

The fifty-milers competed in a variety of weight classes. There are many ways to win in endurance, and that is one of its appeals. There are winners on time in each weight class. Then, from among the top-ten finishers, a best-conditioned victor is chosen by the veterinarians. That trophy is much coveted, testimony to the orientation of the riders around the welfare of the animals. To win a best-conditioned award is also proof of the many hours of riding spent preparing for competition.

The vet-check area of this race exuded horse care. There was a conspicuous water tank, for dehydration is a recognized enemy of equine as well as human athletes today (a welcome improvement from the days our football coaches ran us in pads on hot days, shoving salt tablets at us but prohibiting water). On their mandatory halts, riders had unsaddled their horses, were walking them out, and were encouraging them to eat a little. When stressed, the gut of the horse will sometimes shut down, and it is important the digestive tract continue to work throughout the day.

Sue and two other veterinarians were busy at work, stethoscopes around

*Water is all-important at an endurance event.*

their necks, giving the horses a thorough checking over. Later, in a rare lull (we discovered the vets work extremely hard at these affairs), Sue was able to come over and give us a good orientation. The fifty-milers had a mandatory forty-minute hold at this station, but more important, the forty minutes did not start until the animal's heart rate lowered to sixty-four beats per minute. The rider who brought a horse to the vet while its heart was still racing was wasting his or her time. Now we understood why most of the riders were coming in at a walk and why some were choosing to lead their horses in.

When a horse meets the sixty-four-beat requirement, the vet does a thorough check. A pinch of the skin, preferably on the point of the

*Much of endurance riding takes place in beautiful, rugged country.*

*Smart endurance riders often lead their horses into the vet check area, since their enforced waiting period begins when the animal's heart rate lowers to sixty-four beats per minute.*

A large percentage of endurance riders are women. No specific headgear was required in this event, but helmets are a good idea.

A rider sweet-talks her mare during a rest stop. Although many breeds do well in endurance riding, the Arabian dominates.

shoulder, is a good, quick test for dehydration. If the horse is completely hydrated, the skin will spring back immediately. If the skin comes back in from one half second to one second, some dehydration has taken place, but an acceptable amount. Like humans, horses are sweating animals, so under stress there is always some moisture deficit. If, however, the skin-recovery time gets up to two seconds or more, dehydration is severe enough that the vet will put the horse on hold. If the skin stays distorted, with little inclination to recover, the horse is severely dehydrated and must be placed on I.V.'s. The word of the veterinarian, by the way, is law, and I noticed no arguments whatsoever.

Sue said she also looks for any kind of unsoundness and for an inverted respiratory and heart-rate condition. Some horses pant, and brief stretches when their respiratory rate is higher than their heart rate might be normal for them. But they should recover from that condition quickly.

When the vet is done the forty-minute hold begins, and riders tend first to their horses, then to themselves. But the riders are not cleared to take off on the next leg until they return to the veterinarian for a sound-ness check. Leading their horses, the riders trot off, the horse trotting with them, while the vet looks critically for any favoring of a leg, hip, shoulder, or foot. Only when the horses pass may the rider mount up and head for the hills again.

Twice, during the course of the fifty-mile race, the horses undergo this thorough check. Then, one hour after completing the race, another ex-haustive evaluation is done by the veterinarian, the results being used to clear the riders for placement both on time and for best-conditioned awards. It does no good to win the race on time if your horse is in such poor condition afterwards that it is disqualified.

I was impressed by the whole process. The care of the horses is meticu-lous, and the attitude riders *must* possess toward them is impressive. Riders put the comfort of their horses first. That such a high percentage of endurance riders are women might surprise anyone with lingering stereo-types about the "weaker sex." Women excel in this rough-and-tumble com-petition, in these races that involve rough terrain, galloping a considerable percentage of the day, riding hard for fifty miles each day for three days straight. And at the Bull Mountain ride, who won the race one day, the best-conditioned award one day, and the best-conditioned combined award for all three days? A fifty-seven-year-old woman. Her secrets, according to

Sue, are not stressing the horse, knowing just what it can do, and staying right at that perfect point.

There is, incidentally, a less stressful sport that many try as an introduction to endurance competition, called competitive trail. In this sport there is no race. Riders have parameters—minimum and maximum times—to arrive at checkpoints. Points are given for condition and for care of the horse. Again, the veterinarian is a major player in the event. Horses in competitive trail can compete at age four, a year younger than in endurance, and riders must stay mounted. They are not allowed to lead occasionally as endurance riders are.

Perhaps some of us simply crave competition. One of my sons can make a point-garnering game out of virtually anything, and he has been that way since he was two or three. For such people the solo adventure may not be the right thing. Conquering that mountain trail alone may not be enough. Having others see the accomplishment, share it, and lend their support and society may be the enhancement needed. Endurance riding offers all of that along with intense interaction with a fine horse for miles and miles of fast trail under the big sky.

# Chapter 9

# Solo Trekking on Horseback

I was riding on a wagon road, two parallel trails, through country that would have seemed beautiful had not icy rainwater infiltrated the edges of my poncho and knifed down my back. I realized my right hand had gone completely numb, then understood why. Hunched in the saddle, I held the lead rope to my packhorse Sugar under my right hand, dallied (wrapped) once around the saddle horn, my hand on top of the horn. The brim of my hat was catching rainwater, and the depression in its front acted as a rain gutter to spill a steady stream of chilling water onto my hand—thus the numbness.

The horses themselves were game, far more than I was, and they proceeded in an easy, ground-covering flat walk. Both were Tennessee Walking Horses, sorrels, only three years old, awfully young to be trusted with a jaunt such as this, but proven already. Major, the larger, I rode, while Emily's horse Sugar carried a Decker pack saddle and two plywood boxes, mantied up, containing all I needed to survive by myself for several days longer than I planned to be gone.

But at that point, riding north up the valley of Slough Creek in Yellowstone Park, knowing that the park boundary eleven miles away was really only the start of my journey, soaked, cold, a little depressed at the parting with wife and sons a half hour earlier, I was hardly the picture of the stalwart adventurer. I presented a brave face to the occasional fly fisherman (the number of people would thin out and eventually disappear in the wilderness to the north). The mule packer I met told me my horses were pretty, and I gave him a smile and compliment in return. But in truth I was physically miserable and mentally shaky. Why was I doing this? Why was I tackling a trip across true wilderness during an odd, cold summer when some of the mountain trails had not yet emerged from snow banks, when we had been forced (this very morning, mind you, in *July*) to stop on top of the Beartooth Highway and wait for the snowplow before we could proceed into Cooke City? Why was I tempting fate with a middle-aged body, still newly recovered from a ski accident and a second, horse-related one? Why was I leaving comfort and security for a taste of the unknown, even under relatively controlled, safety-conscious conditions?

Truthfully, I don't know why. "Proving oneself" is something we associate with younger people. I have had plenty of opportunities to do so, have been reasonably satisfied with my "performance," have survived a war and the usual run of stresses and sorrows. But perhaps we don't outlive the necessity to occasionally test our metal. In William Faulkner's "The Bear," a group of men and boys yearly chase an extraordinarily large bear, almost fearing the day the chase will end and their tradition will stop. Once when the dogs close in on "Old Ben" (the bear), a smallish female hound, not known for her bravery, rushes to the front of the fray and attacks. She is terribly wounded.

In camp later, Sam Fathers, the half-black, half-Indian huntsman, explains to the boy Ike why the dog did it:

> . . . *Sam daubed the tattered ear and the raked shoulder with turpentine and axle grease, [while] to the boy it was still no living creature, but the wilderness which, leaning for the moment down, had patted lightly once the hound's temerity.*
>
> *"Just like a man," Sam said. "Just like folks. Put off as long as she could having to be brave, knowing all the time that sooner or later she would have to be brave to keep on living with herself, and knowing all the time beforehand what was going to happen to her when she done it."*

*The author's Tennessee Walking Horse gelding, Major, here at age four, was only three when he made the solo trek from Yellowstone Park over the mountains and home.*

In other words, she has to do it just so she can go on calling herself a dog. Most of us feel no need to challenge nature so violently, so nearly fatally. But many of us need to touch occasionally its power, to shoot rapids in a canoe or climb a cliff, and thus remeasure ourselves.

As in Faulkner's story, we prize wilderness not because it is devoid of man but because it contains that power to measure us. To tackle it alone as I was doing on this trip was not to challenge it but to submerge myself into it, to test my strength against its ebb and flow, to search its dark shadows, to prove that cut from civilization's tether I swim quite well indeed. And through it all there was, in a 360-degree panorama, its beauty.

So to be soaked to the skin and shivering with the beginnings of hypothermia was not an unusual or unexpected state. The wilderness did not owe me any warmth, after all. It was my job to be prepared, and I was. In a waterproof bag behind my saddle was extra warmth I could don (and shortly would, if this continued). With me were all the usual items of safety, the first-aid kit, extra food, shelter, and fire-building materials. And earlier I had made a decision that was conservative and, I believe, wise.

We had traveled by pickup and horse trailer that morning over the highway famed news commentator Charles Kuralt called the most beautiful in the world, the Beartooth Highway, on switchbacks over the top of the world, where we had encountered the July snowstorm. My original plan did not include a launch in Yellowstone Park. We had turned from Cooke City up a logging road to the north, climbed to 9,000 feet in elevation, and stopped next to the parking lot at the trailhead where I'd intended to jump off. The parking lot itself was a giant snowdrift, and flakes of snow blew angrily in the wind. The departure point was a ledge trail down the side of the mountain, which disappeared into fog mixed with thickly falling snow.

Falling snow is often beautiful, but in this case, at high elevation, blanketing a trail probably not yet cleared this season, on a mountainside where turning the horses around could be difficult, it was not beautiful, it was stark reality. It was a bruiser with a threatening look on his face saying, "Try me if you dare." Had I *needed* to travel this way I would have done so. But this trip was for recreation. I scanned the map and decided on the alternate route, a drive first through the northeast entrance of Yellowstone Park to the trailhead at the mouth of Slough Creek (the creek I had intended to reach by crossing another drainage). The elevation marks on the map suggested that my first day, at least, would be below the snowline, and a promising weather forecast might bail me out the day after.

It is difficult to discuss the world's most famous national park with those who have never been there. Take away the word *national* and the first meaning of *park* in my dictionary is "a tract of land for public use in or near a city, usually laid out with walks, drives, playgrounds, athletic fields, etc." In our western mountains the word *park* means a clearing or meadow surrounded by forest. Neither meaning prepares one for a gigantic tract of wild land, larger than several American states and European countries. I have heard advocates for reintroduction of the wolf to Yellowstone Park counter stockmen's objections by asserting that the park should be fenced, thus preventing the escape of the animals into neighboring herds of sheep and cattle. Such innocent souls have no inkling of the immensity of this tract nor of its extreme topography.

At 3,472 square miles (over two million acres or about nine hundred thousand hectares), Yellowstone is around half the size of the state of Israel. True, millions of visitors crowd its geysers and canyon overlooks, but hike off the roads and trails just a few miles and you're in extraordinarily rugged country. The Slough Creek trailhead and its nearby campground were crowded with tourists that morning as I saddled Major and, with help from the boys, adjusted the mantied cargo boxes on Sugar. But I knew that my transition from the overcrowded to the primitive would take place in the space of a couple of hours.

The name "Slough Creek" itself was music to my ears. Many years ago, on a hot July day, my brother and I, both teenagers, were laboring atop a haystack in south-central Montana. We'd stripped off our shirts several hours earlier, and the gallon water jug had been refilled at least once. Our boss, Morris, brought us another load of hay bales with the loader on his tractor, then shut it down to have a drink of water himself. Steve and I sat perched on the edge of the stack, enjoying the relative quiet left behind by the tractor's engine and the hint of a breeze that cooled the sweat on our bodies.

"You know where I'd like to be right now, Steve?" Morris asked, looking up and squinting against the sun, addressing the question to my younger brother in his teasing way. "I'd like to be back up on Slough Creek with a camp in the shade. I'd fish till it warmed up, then lie down on a cot and have a good nap. And these damn hay bales would be the furthest things from my mind."

We knew Morris had been a guide and outfitter and had packed into the mountains many times. High in these dryland hills, especially from the top of the haystack, Steve and I could see the Beartooth Mountains, thirty miles away but on a good day so blue and sharp you felt you could reach out from the haystack and touch them. And looking toward the southwest we could follow the line of Morris's arm and see approximately where Slough Creek would be.

And yet, though I'd reached my late forties and spent much time in the mountains, I had never experienced the shade of Slough Creek. Well, I was going now, snow and rain be damned, and Major hit a running walk like a Tennessee show horse in that crowded parking lot. When we reached the trail sign, we looked back for a wave at Em and the boys, then headed north.

I mentioned a wagon road at the beginning of this chapter, and I should explain. To the north of Yellowstone Park lies the Absaroka-Beartooth wilderness area, a vast tract of mountains and forest in which development and machines with engines are prohibited. However, a private ranch, the Silvertip, is located just across the border. Its existence predates the wilderness area, thus it is "grandfathered" legally, able to continue as a commercial, privately owned operation. Its only access, though, is from Yellowstone Park and this same trailhead at which I'd launched my journey, and the ranch is serviced by horse and wagon. I had noticed a team of horses pulling a buckboard with several guests aboard earlier, and now I rode on this unusual double trail, this wilderness road that allowed no motor vehicles, only an occasional wagon from the Silvertip Ranch.

Had the rain continued during that soggy trip north toward the park boundary, I'm certain I would have coped. But two things happened simultaneously. First I saw the moose, a huge bull, knee-deep in the creek, and second, I saw a glint of sunlight off his sleek black hide. The storm broke just that quickly. Then Major spotted the moose, a new creature in his lexicon, this pseudo-horse with horns, and we had a lively ride for a quarter mile, my colt in reluctant control, trying to find a route his master would allow to give the strange creature the widest possible berth.

The moose ignored us, plunging his nose repeatedly into the shallows for whatever nourishment he was finding. Then he raised his head, eyed the far side of Slough Creek, crossed as effortlessly as a gigantic bird, and trotted away. Major, Sugar, and I, now that the horses' breathing was normal and the snorts had stopped, found a sunlit clearing. I dismounted, retrieved a sandwich, and ate it lovingly, the sun now warm on my face. A nagging back problem had added to my earlier discomfort, but it was oddly better now, and the horses nuzzled the ground for grass, steam rising from their wet hides. It was all better now.

Back in the saddle, an occasional trail sign counting down the distance to the park boundary, I rode with less and less company. Few fly fisherman had ventured this far from the parking lot, and soon, suddenly, there was no one at all on the trail.

If I were H. Ross Perot and it were for sale (it is *not*), I would buy the Silvertip Ranch. An old-fashioned guest ranch of the very most splendid style, the ranch sits by a bend in Slough Creek, its buildings of logs stained brown, its atmosphere that of quiet class in a wilderness setting. It does *not* currently operate as a public guest ranch, however, so don't bother inquiring about staying there. It's managed only for the pleasure of its owners and their friends.

I stopped at the sign saying I was leaving Yellowstone Park, balking for a moment at the idea of entering private land. The trail appeared to cross the horse pasture to the right of the buildings. Time for another map consultation. Before the trip I had invested in an aftermarket map that was covered with a plastic material for waterproofing. It was expensive, but it had already proven its worth, for a conventional paper map would have been a lump of pulp by now. Even this improved version was already showing signs of wear.

At this point I noticed two cowboys to my left, saddling a horse in front of the barn. Rather than trespass indiscriminately I rode down the lane toward them, said hello and asked where I should go to pick up the forest service trail to the north. One of the men gestured toward the pasture and said, "Right across there." Neither was friendly in the usual western sense. At first I resented that, then decided they may have had reason when the second man asked me, as I turned to go, "Those other guys are camped up above, then?"

"I'm alone," I said. Their stiff manner immediately eased, and I said "Take care." I can only assume a party that had made themselves somewhat unwelcome had passed earlier, and the cowboys initially assumed I was connected with them.

So, my horses snorty at the smells and sounds of new buildings, people, and animals, we passed through the Silvertip Ranch, found the trail outlet, and paused on higher ground to rest, look back, and take pictures. Sugar was packing a grain sack on top of the Decker between the two manties. It kept sloughing off to one side, then the other. I fixed it, mentally noting that the next morning, when the sack was lightened by an evening's rations, I would manty it up in one pack or the other, shifting cargo as necessary.

It had been nearly noon when I parted with Emily, Jon, and Steve, and now the afternoon was wearing on. The ache in my back had returned along with a touch of loneliness; the idea of a snug campsite with cheery fire had appeal. My map showed a mile or so of timber as the valley bottom narrowed, then a broadening of the valley with open parks and meadows and a Forest Service cabin. I would find and pass the cabin, then look for a campsite on the relatively flat valley bottom to the north. But before getting there I would have one of my last encounters with people before two days of solitude, an encounter just a little mysterious.

I spotted them before they saw me, two men on horseback, by dress and manner and riding ability obviously a middle-aged "dude" (paying guest) and a bearded guide riding in front of him. The guide rode with that easy slouch of familiarity with the saddle. He looked up and saw me as I reined Major to the right at a broad place in the trail. We would stop and let them pass.

As he drew closer I recognized the guide, in spite of his beard, as a man I'd known years earlier, a man who had fought and eventually won a long court battle with a government agency but who had lost his outfitter's license in the process. When the head of his Appaloosa drew even, he looked me in the face and said, "You're Dan Aadland, aren't you. Remember me? I'm Ron ————." The name he gave was *not* the one by which I'd known him, definitely not his, for I knew his father and family. "Plenty of nice campsites up ahead. Your horses look good. Well, we won't hold you up." It was all said rapidly, in a good-natured but businesslike fashion. Then they were gone down the trail.

The whole thing happened too quickly for me to react, and then I felt a little conned. What the man had done was quite sensible. Faced with a former acquaintance on the trail, someone who might say his name, he beat me to the punch, gambling that I would be taken aback or cooperative or simply reluctant to correct a man's statement of his own name. It was obvious to me that he was operating under an alias and that he did not want his paying guest to know.

Now there was nothing dangerous about this encounter, but it alerted me just the same. The wilderness will still occasionally draw a shady character. I know a man who camped for an entire summer not far from where I was now riding, with only one purpose—to evade the IRS. And that brings up a subject we just cannot avoid when discussing the joys of going solo in the backcountry. I may have been statistically safer on this backcountry trip than I would have been walking across Central Park after dark, but that does not alter that fact that had *anything* gone wrong on so remote a trip I would have been in serious trouble. There was no 911 number to call.

Mention safety on a trip like mine and the urban dweller is likely to think first of dangerous animals. That concern was certainly a relevant one in this case, for I was in grizzly country. True, chances of an encounter were unlikely, of an encounter I couldn't avoid less likely yet. I consider it foolish to travel unarmed in true grizzly country, but I was on the fringes of it and travel through a national park prohibits packing a firearm. Less threatening creatures like moose can, on rare occasions, be dangerous also. The proper posture toward any of them is respect, not fear, but remember they are not sweet Disney creatures that pose no danger if you simply treat them kindly.

The potential for a dangerous encounter with a human being, as with an animal, is slight in the backcountry, but it does exist. Defense decisions are highly personal ones, but one should certainly be aware and watchful. Virtually all the people you meet in the backcountry are there for the same reasons you are, and they are fine people. But it's foolish to ignore the possibility you could meet someone who did not fit that description.

Still, accidents pose the greatest potential danger for the backcountry traveler, especially if he or she is traveling alone. Fall off a curb and break an ankle in the city, and help is relatively close. Hurt yourself the same way on a trip like this one of mine and it could conceivably cost your life. The sharpest difference is simply the availability and proximity of help. A slip with your pocket knife that causes a relatively minor cut requiring a couple of stitches under normal circumstances would now become a major and demoralizing problem. Even if your first-aid kit were complete and you were cool enough to use it well, all chances of really enjoying the trip would be over. You would be too strained and uncomfortable working around the injury while packing and doing camp chores.

The truly serious accidents, the smashed leg when a horse slips and goes down on the rider, create almost unthinkable survival situations. Don't get me wrong, they *can be* and frequently *are* survived, but the ordeals created are relished by no one. I've evolved a personal system I'll share with you. First, I do some real thinking about just what level of risk is acceptable. All risk cannot be eliminated in any activity, and to tackle a trip solo is to accept the fact that no matter what preparations you make some risk remains. A twenty-one-year-old rock climber has, we hope, recognized a certain level of risk as acceptable. So has a solo sailor who is fifty-five.

Secondly, it's essential that people who care about you know your route and your tentative itinerary. True, it may dampen your sense of freedom to follow a schedule when it precludes that twenty-four-hour jaunt to an unplanned lake, but the specter of lying hurt somewhere no one would think to look makes the trade-off more than fair for me. I always leave Emily a map marked with felt tip of both the trail I intend to follow and one or more alternative routes. After all, you can't predict a washed-out bridge or trail, and you may have to resort to "Plan B." (That happened on this trip.)

Thirdly, preparation must include a first-rate first-aid kit, more than a pack of Band-Aids, and the knowledge to use it. Wound sutures and perhaps even prescription painkillers might be in order. Your personal physician should be your guide in assembling this "superkit." There are excellent medical guides available, some targeting small-boat sailors, a fiercely independent group who take medical preparation extremely seriously. I'm assuming, of course, awareness of other safety equipment needs, fire starters, extra warmth, perhaps signal panels for making an SOS visible from the air, as well as a compass, relevant maps, and a thorough knowledge of land navigation. A surprising number of backcountry travelers are now packing cellular phones (irony of ironies, since we're trying get *away* from phones), and some rescues have resulted. However, such phones are often useless in deep mountain valleys, and if you're hurt or injured you probably won't be able to climb to a mountaintop from which their signal can be heard. Also, battery life is quite limited in most models.

Lastly, and perhaps most important of all, you must modify your behavior when alone in the wilderness. A modest activity, well within risk parameters when you are with others who could help you, might be well outside acceptable risk when you are alone. A climb to a high point off the trail to see the view; an enjoyable gallop through a meadow; a ford over a questionable stretch of river; all these might tip the scales unacceptably on a solo trip. You begin, if you follow this process, to sound like your own nagging parent, but that's as it should be. When alone you *need* that cautious "superego" to keep you in line.

This was far from the first solo trip for me, yet I found myself taking pains over the most mundane things. Mounting my saddle horse with the lead of my packhorse in hand became an activity carefully planned to avoid the slight chance of tangling my leg in the line and having a wreck should the horses spook. I was more cautious than usual with fire and particularly so with my small ax, a tool I consider at least as hazardous as a firearm.

But all this concern with safety and potential for disaster should not dampen your spirit. It should function more as a conscience, an underlying awareness of reality. I don't remember it spoiling my quiet, tired enjoyment of the last portion of that first day's ride, that easy walk up a tree-lined trail, the horses tired but willing, the scenery as beautiful and mysterious as a medieval forest that could hold trolls or leprechauns. We found the Forest Service maintenance cabin where the valley began to widen, where it opened into meadows and scattered timber, flat, country begging to be camped in. I had no interest in stopping at the cabin, not for more than a moment to rest the horses without dismounting; then I moved on, satisfied with the verification of my progress it provided.

As the mysterious man had said, there were many fine campsites ahead. Only now did I fully understand the longing of my haying boss, years ago, for this green valley, its cool shade and clear stream. Averaging perhaps a half mile wide, the valley bottom was thinly timbered, with much open space. Good grass was everywhere, as were outfitters' campsites that had not been used since last fall's hunting season. These were marked by stashes of seasoned lodgepoles, used for setting up tents, and occasionally semipermanent fireplaces, built before "no-trace" fire building became the method of choice. I had my pick of sites and soon settled on a half-acre patch of grass with a trio of stately pines in the middle of the meadow, cooperatively located so that I could string a manty tarp as a canopy and set up my cooking area underneath.

When I recall the area now, the color green, in many shades, comes first to mind. This is quite remarkable. Five years earlier, in the drought year of 1988, a force marched up this valley and south into Yellowstone Park, a force as destructive as divisions of enemy soldiers, white hot with rage. The force was a terrible series of forest fires that devastated much of Yellowstone Park and the surrounding wilderness, which threatened the town of Cooke City and nearly destroyed the Silvertip Ranch, through which I had just passed. There were many fires that summer, and when crews the size of military divisions were dispatched to fight one of them, lightning simply struck tinder-dry timber in another region and a fire started there.

Forest fires are paradoxical. We have been taught by generations of Smokey Bear commercials that forest fires are bad. A half-century of fire suppression, however, had made "the big one" all the more inevitable, for deadfall had accumulated on the forest floor, creating a colossal fuel supply for the eventual disaster. Then came the summer of 1988, one of the driest on record, and the forest literally exploded.

But here is the paradox: Scientists, nearly universally, say fire is good, that it causes a great rejuvenation. Cones of the lodgepole pine lie dormant on the forest floor until fire opens them up, liberates their seed. Fire thins the stands of timber and lets sunlight through. Further, since most fires in this area are caused by lightning, fire is "natural." Thus, in a rare instance of science having its way with politics, the management of western forests had developed a "let it burn" policy before 1988, had shifted away from Smokey Bear, and many blamed that change for the catastrophe. From what I could see that summer, I disagreed. The policy may have slowed initial reaction to the first fires, but then total mobilization took place. It was a battle between nature and man, and nature had all the cards.

Our family was camped by the Stillwater River, my destination on this later solo trip, on July 2, 1988. We watched a small forest fire eat its way up the near-vertical valley wall across the river, the fire fingering out between the rock outcroppings, impossible to fight with people on the ground. We learned that fire jumped the river a couple of days later, trapping two hikers who saved themselves only by sinking into the cold river water.

Now, in 1993, any lingering doubts I had about the biologists' side of the controversy were settled in my mind. Everywhere around me nature was repairing the damage, sparkling green under newfound sunshine. Everywhere were thickets of new trees, knee-high, and where fire had scorched the old trees most mercilessly, the new growth of grass and seedlings was most lush. True, I would regret that the cycle of nature is slow, that during my lifetime I would never again see parts of these valleys under the stately timber I'd seen a few years ago. I would tire of sooty lead

*The author's solo camp on Slough Creek.*

ropes, of manty tarps turned black from Sugar rubbing his packs against the singed tree trunks. But I would watch this magnificent terrain flaunt its new, sunny beauty, and end up feeling the biologists were right. (Ironically, as I write this, Smokey Bear is back in force on the radio commercials I hear each day. One of T. S. Eliot's characters said, "Humankind cannot bear too much reality.")

But on the flat valley bottom near Slough Creek, in a clearing with deep grass, already being tested by Major and Sugar, I could with complete satisfaction make my camp. True, much work was involved. A solo pack trip leaves no one with whom you can divide up the chores. All horse wrangling, tent pitching, and cooking must be done by yourself. First I unsaddled the horses, carrying Sugar's packs to the area I would call home (and from which the horses were barred). Then I rewarded both animals with a ration of grain followed by a picket line long enough to allow grazing. Always, I take care of my horses first.

The timberline tent went up quickly, and since the weather was unsettled, anything water-sensitive went inside. I strung a manty tarp from trees over a flat stump, a perfect table, and only then put on the coffeepot. Late afternoon sun played peek-a-boo with the clouds, while I sipped a beer, waiting for the coffee to perk. I heard the bell of a packhorse turned loose to graze and realized I was not alone in the valley. Though their camp was not in sight, a packing party was in the area, and their large horse herd passed later near my camp.

It seems trite, yet true, to recall the pungency of food cooked outdoors, in this case lean Polish sausages made of elk meat, with noodles boiling on the side, then fruit from a small can for dessert, simple, elegant. I had not realized how hungry I was. With utensils cleaned up I headed toward the creek with fly rod in one hand and a small saucepan in the other. I would fill the pan with water to be pumped through my filter and into my canteen. About the fishing I really wasn't serious. I had plenty of food to eat and am not an enthusiastic catch-and-release fisherman. I would rather catch to keep and eat where it is ecologically sound and legally permissible. When that is not appropriate, I would just as soon do other things. "Big fish eat little fish," as the saying goes, and there is nothing wrong with being the big fish. But I'm less enthusiastic about putting fish repeatedly through the process of conversion from creature to protein in the pan when the process exists merely as a game.

Well, the conflict never surfaced because no fish did either. They were as casual about the whole affair as I was, and after a little casting practice I filled my pan and picked my way through the coming dusk to camp. Once there I built up my fire, lit my small backpacking lantern, and took out the notebook journal I had started at suppertime in the form of a letter to Emily. Here are some excerpts:

> *Keeping both a journal and a letter to you will probably not be possible, so I'll combine them. I'm sitting a couple hundred yards from Slough Creek in a nearly flat valley bottom, with thin tree cover. Most of the trees are fire scarred. It's very beautiful here. When I arrived the sun was actually out, but the first two hours after the trailhead were ridden in solid, heavy rain.*
>
> *Now it's getting stormy again. . . . Frankly, I'm having a little trouble keeping my morale up, with the wet weather, nervous start, etc. I just saw a hummingbird. He came up to the cooking area, hovered looking it over, then left!*

*The "kitchen."*

    *We're camped upstream from the Slough Creek Work Station and only a short distance from where Wolverine Creek comes in. That's where I'd have descended had I left from Daisy Pass. We traveled perhaps fourteen miles. The horses are very tired. They've been angels, though Sugar gets lazy sometimes and needs a pull. We've traveled mostly in a slow flat walk.*

    *I just fished for a few minutes (nothing was interested), filled a couple water cans, and came back to the fire. I got wet to above my knees walking through wet brush, but the fire is doing well, and I'll dry out.*

    *A whole herd of horses, some with bells, just passed camp, and two mule deer just bounded through. This is a perfect camp! It's so ideal I felt depressed when I first arrived that our whole family wasn't along. Some day we'll all get over here. . . .*

    *Nick Adams [Hemingway's character] went fishing alone because the war had broken his body and spirit, and he felt simplifying his existence, taking a step at a time with simple tasks, could restore him in time. He was doing an emergency version of Thoreau. I'm in much better shape than Nick was, but I'm not as I was five years ago. Some physical problems, the losses . . . have combined with a few more years on the tally. . . . Perhaps I am doing something a little like Nick Adams did. And just as he wasn't quite ready to fish the swamp in "Big Two-Hearted River," I wasn't quite ready to jump off at Daisy Pass in the snowstorm. [In the next day's entry I would say that I had over-intellectualized in comparing my situation to Nick's, that I truly like doing this sort of thing, the adventure and challenge, even if I'm not happy all of the time and am lonely much of it.]*

When writer's cramp set in (it does soon, so dependent I am on computer keys), I snuffed the lantern to sit on my camp stool by the fire a while. It was still too cloudy for a good look at the stars, but the river was audible and a coyote howled. Then I checked the picketed horses one last time, and by light of my tiny flashlight went into the tent, found my sleeping bag, and sank into its warmth. When I closed my eyes the trail continued by me in my mind's eye just like the view I'd had all day between Major's ears. But not for long. I soon slept.

*Day Two.* It rained only a little during the night, and morning dawned with partial sun. I crawled out of my tent, checked to see that Major and Sugar were still where they belonged, then eyed the distant peaks uneasily. Some were catching morning sun, while others were shrouded in clouds, clouds that meant falling snow. All routes from here to home (except the one back into Yellowstone) involved passes higher than nine thousand feet, and the snowline yesterday had been a thousand feet lower than that. I did not relish tackling a trail not yet used this season, on a mountain ledge trail over a pass that high. I would hope for the best.

The anxiety was certainly not enough to spoil my morning, however. The coffee smelled great as it perked, and it tasted even better. My breakfast omelet turned out beautifully, and the horses seemed game and fit. I moved things along quickly. This would be the longest day of travel (though I had no idea it would become *that* long); I had many miles to go before I'd sleep.

Even after one day the packs were lighter. The horses had eaten enough grain to allow mantying the grain sack as planned; I'd consumed food and some canned beer and soft drinks. All traces of fatigue were gone from

Major and Sugar. They were ready to get at it. After my last policing of the campsite I swung into the saddle and Major hit a silky running walk, his neck arched, "looking for the next town," as the old-timers used to say. Indeed, he and Sugar both were right on the edge, right at that point where a bit more spirit would be dangerous, but still completely in control. A good saddle horse moving like that is the Lamborghini of the experienced rider. There is no greater joy.

We flew through the scattered timber and rejoined the trail, which soon took us across a broad flat to a ford over Slough Creek. I now noticed a large outfitter's camp at the timber's edge on the west side of the valley about half a mile away. Closer to us, still in yellow slicker in case the rain should resume, was a lone horseman, casually sitting his horse. We splashed through the creek and headed toward him, my horses snorty, ready to spook if they could find an excuse, both eyeing the man, his horse, and the yellow garment that flapped in the morning breeze. I reined in twenty yards from the man, and we exchanged pleasantries. He was out enjoying the morning, casually keeping an eye out for two of the camp's fishermen to check when they would be back for breakfast. "Nice horses," he said.

I told him where we were going, that one of my excuses for crossing the mountains was to give the young Walker colts some experience. "They sure move out," he said with a smile. "It won't take you long to get there." Then I gave Major a slight squeeze with my knees, and we scooted off north on the trail toward the high passes. The outfitter would be the last human I would see until I arrived at the trailhead on the Stillwater.

Shortly after we crossed the broad sage flat by Slough Creek, the valley narrowed and we were back in the timber again. All the trees around us were fire damaged in varying degrees, but the grass under them was lush. We passed another semipermanent outfitter's camp, this one deserted for the time being, then were completely alone, the trail temporarily rising on the side of the valley, the sound of Slough Creek now gone.

Suddenly I was looking at elk. We had entered a small, boggy clearing with one large tree in the center. Two cow elk were watching me, one bedded, the other standing, trying to decide whether to gather up their calves and run. They were uneasy but not terribly afraid. Although Slough Creek is a favorite elk-hunting area in the fall, the two cows seemed to know it was the wrong time of year for hunters to covet elk steaks and chops. My 35mm camera had hung on the saddle horn from the time we launched, even through the rain, and I brought it out now. I had mounted an all-purpose lens, a 28mm to 80mm zoom, with too little telephoto capability to produce close-ups of the animals, even though they were only fifty yards away, but I hoped for usable photos of them. (The resulting pictures turned out quite nicely.)

I had decided to progress to the trail junction where the Wounded Man Trail (named after a lake and creek that were named after, I assume, an unfortunate human being) turned to the right. There I would eat a sandwich and gear myself for the climb over the pass. I made map checks frequently, perhaps every half hour, now and then checking the compass azimuth. I'm as uncomfortable as a sea captain with any uncertainty of my location. That trait would later prove a valuable one, for never since my Marine Corps days had I relied more on my map, compass, and ability to use them.

By late morning, in a pretty meadow just past another ford over Slough Creek, I reached the long-awaited trail junction. Before I could celebrate, however, I noticed the weathered Forest Service trail sign: "Wounded Man Trail No. 309" and under that, "Trail Not Maintained." In solemn verification I looked where the trail should have been, at the avenue through the trees to the northeast, and noticed the grass was deep on the trail. Nothing had passed there this summer, and use for several years must have been little or none. This was a serious development. The sign meant the trail was not annually "logged," cleared of the deadfall that normally accumulates from year to year. Since the fires had caused far more than the normal quantity of trees falling across the trail, this would likely mean several years' accumulation, and it would be improbable that horses could pass at all in some places. Sometimes it is easy enough to detour around fallen trees, but on slide areas, for instance, it can be impossible. I didn't relish the idea of sawing my way clear to the Stillwater drainage.

"Not maintained" meant other things as well. Washed-out trail bridges would not have been replaced, and the entire trail could disappear under a slide on a steep mountain slope. Had I been backpacking I may have attempted the trail anyway, but I doubted whether even then I would have done so alone. There was nothing to do but accept Plan B. That involved backtracking a mile or so and heading east up the mountain toward Horseshoe Lake. Certainly the route would be as beautiful, so I accepted the change without too much disappointment.

Shortly before noon, the horses confused with the change of direction, I found the second junction. The trail was actually an old mining road, a "cat" (bulldozer) trail remaining from mining days before this area was designated as wilderness. I heard later that an old bulldozer was driven down this trail the very last day it was legal. For a trail the old road was quite luxurious, though steep. I had trouble finding a place level enough for the horses to rest easily while tied, but eventually did, then sat on a boulder and ate my lunch. The weather was still unsettled, white clouds sailing rapidly across the blue sky, occasionally with misting rain, then clearing again.

After lunch we climbed rapidly, and the horses began to tire. We rested frequently. The timber began to thin. The trees at this elevation had not been burned, the grass was good, the green lush in the alpine clearings we now reached. Perhaps I lost concentration just once as the dozer road petered out, perhaps a conventional trail had veered off somewhere on the mountain. Whichever the case, I soon faced a ridge with no visible trail. Horseshoe Lake simply had to be on the other side, but there was no getting there on any trail I could see. I backtracked several times, made Major and Sugar regain the same elevation, found myself for the first time that day (it would not be the last) having trouble concentrating on the puzzle at hand, far from panic, true, but understanding why that emotion is such a common sand trap for people in this sort of situation.

I studied my map and compass many times. Once I did a resection using the Slough Creek valley, which I could see clearly to the south into Yellowstone, for one bearing and two mountain peaks I could be relatively certain about toward the north, for the others. One reverses the azimuths and draws them on the map. My location was where the lines on the map crossed. Okay, I was just where the terrain features around me made me think I was. But where was the trail? This I knew, that Horseshoe Lake simply had to be over the ridge, a ridge ninety-eight hundred feet in elevation. Finally I decided the ridge could be climbed by both the horses and me if I walked rather than rode. Now the incredible dispositions of the two colts really came to play. Both stayed mellow and cooperative as if understanding something was wrong, that they needed to let me concentrate. I tied Sugar's lead rope to the saddle horn on Major with a quick-release knot and headed up the ridge.

Naturally, since in mountains one can never see the true crest from below but is seeing what the marines call the "military crest," there was another ridge above the first one, but it too was climbable. Finally, my lungs burning, the air thin and chilly, we were there, on the ridge, looking down at Horseshoe Lake. This absolute verification of my position was most welcome, but it did not solve all my problems. The lake was five hundred feet below me, nearly straight down. Never mind. I now knew the trail *had* to wrap around this ridge to the north, and I struck an angle in that direction.

Yes, it was there. Another dozer trail curved around the north end of the ridge, but this time there was another problem, snow, lots of it, banks a hundred yards long over the top of the trail forming steep side hills offering questionable traction. Would the horses sink in the snow, some of which must have been eight or ten feet deep? Or would the compacted stuff hold us on top but with slippery footing? The thought of an uncontrollable slide down one of the banks and off the nearly vertical drop at the base of the snow was too terrible to contemplate. I would test the footing gingerly, get off and lead if it proved touchy, turn back in defeat if it were impassable. Relief came when I saw that Major and Sugar sank in about six inches, not enough to make travel exhausting for them but more than enough to afford excellent traction.

And so, soon, we rounded the ridge and dropped down the steep dozer trail to an emerald lake which shone in the sun, its surface rippled with the chilly high-altitude breeze. I had read there were brook trout in this lake, but I would not take time to find out. I tied the horses to scrub pines, took a few pictures, ate half a sandwich and drank a Coke. It was three P.M. now, and I had once hoped to be at Lake of the Woods, not far from the Stillwater valley, by this time. But being in too great a hurry caused me to cut a corner, literally, that cost me much frustration and an hour or more lost.

Again the problem involved a trail that petered out, and instead of following approximately where the map said the trail should be, I cut through the timber down the drainage, knowing I would have to rejoin the trail eventually. I did so, but only after getting the horses into some steep boggy stuff (the whole mountainside was a continual spring), having to lead them again over deadfall, and only through blind good luck avoiding sinking one into the spongy ground. Yes, I found the

*Sugar carried the manties all the way. Here, his breast collar has slipped down and needs tightening.*

trail, the horses clipping along now at the relief of going downgrade instead of up.

But soon, again, I could tell something was wrong. The trail should have been winding up the mountainside to the left, not spilling me into this pretty glade by a new creek, this place that beckoned me with the idea of saying hell with it and camping to sort out the land navigation problems in the morning. The "I am nearly lost" feeling returned with a greater chill than it had earlier. Never, through these fits and starts, was I worried about my survival. But I was worried about my schedule. Over it all hung the simple fact that although I was well prepared to stay an extra day or two, although I warned Emily that could happen, I knew full well what worries she would have to wrestle with if I were overdue.

Again, I backtracked. Again, I asked the brave young horses to gain elevation they had sweated over earlier. They quietly complied, and in less time than I feared we found where our tracks had joined the trail from the woods on the left and, just a hundred yards beyond, the trail off to the right that we had missed. Once on it the horses seemed to smell victory; or, perhaps, they gained their second wind. The ascent was smooth and not terribly steep. Major hit a running walk for part of it. Soon I was in still another idyllic mountain meadow, again with vague trails and rock cairns to mark the passage. With only an occasional miscue, we stayed on the trail. Now, to the east, the late sun lighting them up, were magnificent, rarely seen mountain peaks of almost unbelievable ruggedness. Sawtooth Mountain, a massive brick of granite with nearly vertical sides, loomed out of the meadow green several miles to my right, a true hall for a mountain king, a place, I was certain, that virtually no one ever went.

I paused for a picture or two, but never for long. A sense of urgency hovered over me. The long day at high altitude, much of it over nine thousand feet, was perhaps taking its toll. I had a slight headache. I knew that dehydration was the most common cause, that thin, dry, mountain air, winter or summer, tends to extract moisture from the system. I sipped frequently on my canteen, but probably not to the necessary degree. Finally I topped out on a high ridge and peered over it with anticipation. There it was, the valley of Horseshoe Creek, a tributary of the Stillwater River. I had not reached my destination, but now at least I was about to descend into the correct drainage.

This descent I did on foot. There comes a time when one admits to the limitations of muscle and bone, both of his own and of his horses. Major and Sugar showed still a steady willingness. But a steep drop into this valley on a rocky trail would have its hazards. Had the day been young and the horses fresh, I would have ridden down. But now I led Major, again with Sugar's lead tied to the horn. Although leading did not lessen Sugar's load, Major, carrying a heavy man, had been the more stressed. The milder pace, at least, would help Sugar. It felt good, too, to unbend my legs, to feel the muscles work again.

It is amazing how fast one can walk to the bottom of a mountain. We dropped nearly two thousand feet in less than an hour, and soon I could see Lake of the Woods, a possible camping spot, below me. As I contemplated a camp there, the buzz of mosquitoes hovering around my head increased intensity, and I noticed how swampy and uninviting the clearing around the lake appeared.

At this point I made the decision to go all the way down to the Stillwater before I camped. Perhaps it was not a wise decision. Sometimes one gets into a tired momentum, a mind state in which stopping for camp seems an intrusion. Too, I kept thinking how much easier the next day would be if it involved only a scoot sixteen miles down the Stillwater with no mountains to climb, no snow fields to fear. The horses seemed content to move on as well. True, going downhill can be tougher on muscles and joints than going up, but there is no denying that it spares the heart and lungs. Sugar and Major, after their rest, were willing.

My recollection of the rest of the day takes on a dreamy quality. Tired, very tired, I made it down the rocky trail that parallels Horseshoe Creek, rarely now referring to my map (for I was getting near my home country), falsely secure in the perception that good campsites would be easy to find once I reached the Stillwater. I'd forgotten. So I rode and rode, reaching finally the trail junction and turning north, downriver, toward home. The Stillwater River below me was its usual wild self, its roar, whenever the trail veered within a couple hundred yards, threatening yet reassuring.

We pass a moose cow and calf. Major hardly looks this time. Was it just yesterday the bull moose spooked him back in The Park? (Yellowstone Park, during my growing up, was always simply "The Park.") The big colt has learned a great deal since then.

Most of the time the trail passes through steep, rocky, timbered slopes, impossible for camp. Always, I expect better just around the next bend. Twice we glide through clearings I could use, but they are boggy looking, with high grass the horses covet, but the sort of grass that promises soggy ground.

Suddenly, the sun is gone. The light of the long July day will linger a while, but I face the possibility that I will set up camp in darkness. Apparently there are no good campsites until Big Park, just twelve miles from my home trailhead. Before the thought of going all the way to Big Park has a chance to depress me, I look toward the north and feel of flood of recognition, realize I am looking at a familiar mountain on the east valley wall, realize I'm only a mile or so from that campsite I've used many times before.

It is dark when I reach it, the deep grass on a flat place by the roaring, misnamed Stillwater River, just at the spot the bridge used to be before the fire. The river cannot be safely crossed without the bridge, so, since the park lies on the east side of the river, I will not attempt to camp there. It has rained again; it would be hard to build a fire. I'm too tired to enjoy a proper camp. The horses will benefit from this place, though. I picket them to burned tree trunks so they can tear into the grass. My tent goes up; I drink a beer and eat a cheese sandwich left over from lunch. I am altogether too tired to cook, and the hunger I felt several hours earlier is oddly gone. I do enjoy hearing the horses munch in the darkness. They bite big hunks of the tall green grass, yank it loose with a tearing sound, and chew. Though I've been tying both colts short during the night (an American Westerner's greatest phobia is losing his horse), I allow both to stay picketed tonight so they can eat as much as possible.

Too tired to concentrate on writing in my journal, I feel my way through the tent door and into my sleeping bag. Soon, but not instantly, I'm asleep.

· · ·

*An interlude.* Some years before this trip I camped alone in the clearing across the bridge that used to be here, by a Forest Service line cabin that used to be in the clearing. I slept on a tarp in the open under chilly, clear stars. It was my first solo overnight trip, a brief jaunt with my gelding Rockytop, a light camp packed in bags fore and aft of my saddle, just a twelve-mile ride from the trailhead to Big Park and then out the next day. My memories of that trip are vivid. I remember telling someone that the last few miles of the trip up, when I rode slowly on my tired horse, were in country that looked like *The Sound of Music.*

Several years later I returned to Big Park with my middle and youngest sons, Jonathan and Steve. They were on their first pack trip, though I had backpacked with Jon. Steve, ten or so at the time, I entrusted to Mona, a veteran mare who had carried dudes for many years while she was owned by an outfitter. Now, in my sleeping bag, I hear the voices of those boys, hear them fixed at that younger age, hear them play and laugh. I smell the very food we cooked, see the young cow moose that explored our camp-site the next morning. Everything is more poignant in the wilderness. Everything tastes more and smells more and sounds more.

I realize, in these brief moments before sleep overtakes me, that regarding forest fires I cannot face emotionally what I believe biologically. Yes, biologically fire is good. But my hands are sooty from the rubbing of the packs and ropes on burned tree trunks all day. The pack bridge is gone, burned. The pretty cabin, even to its much-vandalized door (there were many names carved there) is gone. The forest itself that surrounded the big clearing (we call clearings "parks" in Montana) is gone, making the park, which is surrounded by naked tree trunks, appear larger and scarcely a park at all. Continuing to call it such seems pointless.

The boys who were with me on that second trip are alive and thriving, but they are not here now, and the point of life at which they were is also gone. I have grown older.

.　　.　　.

*Day Three.* At one A.M. on the third day I experience the one true fright of the trip. I awake terribly ill, weak, close to the point of vomiting, shaky. I crawl to the door of the tent carefully, not wanting to upset any delicate balance, and get my head into the fresh air. The night breeze in my face then begins to work on the stomach, takes it back from the point of no return, cools the lavish sweat on my face. I stay there half through the tent door, letting the wind work on me.

While I struggle physically with this strange, severe, and unexpected illness, I come mentally close to panic. I have imagined, even anticipated, injury from accident, threat from forest fire, and failure of horseflesh. But this weird incapacitation, this unexpected weakness has sneaked up on me. How, right now, could I saddle a horse, put a pack on one, even take down the tent? I let the breeze keep cooling me and gradually feel a slackening. I ease back into my sleeping bag, then find, like a drunken man, the one position where the world does not want to spin. I go, very uneasily, to sleep. In the morning I am a little tender, but fine.

What was it? Was spending most of the day at high elevation related? Was the illness acute mountain sickness (ACM), brought on by dehydration? Or had I eaten something questionable earlier in the day? I had been extremely careful, and I had filtered all my drinking water through a modern device so sophisticated it even blocks the dreaded giardia. Perhaps the malady was at least partially psychological, its symptoms prompted by solitude, worry, physical stress, even the roar of the too-near river. I will probably never know the answer, but there was a sort of triumph at finding myself intact that morning. Though fog socked in the valley and another drizzle had begun, I had an "I-have-come-through" attitude and a keen hunger for some fine breakfast.

The horses that third morning were better than ever. All night they had munched knee-deep grass. I had picketed each to the trunk of a burned tree, just far enough apart to prevent tangling in the other's rope. This length, it turned out, was also just right to allow them to come up and inspect my little kitchen, laid out on an inverted manty box. They both peered into my frying pan at the eggs I was cooking.

As the fog closed in the drizzle began, and I packed up my camp quickly. The manties were lighter now, my routine perfected, and soon I was ready. I took a few minutes to walk up the river, then to look at the site of the old bridge, to superimpose the pre-1988, pre-forest fire pictures on these new ones. It will all come back, yes. If I ever see it looking much like it used to, I will be an old man, and even then the trees will not be as large. Meanwhile, elk will enjoy grass where the lodgepole pines grew so thick the forest floor was sterile, and if I'm lucky, I'll be able to enjoy an occasional wapiti steak.

The drizzle now became rain. I put on my poncho and mounted Major. I knew it would be a wet, cold ride to the trailhead, that my eyeglasses would be fogged much of the time, that the many landmarks in this familiar, twelve-mile stretch would be lost to low visibility. But I was not distressed.

I came to the spot the boys and I had seen the bear on that earlier trip. On the way up we had noticed inverted rocks, big ones, rolled from their beds to expose insects, so we had known there was a bear. On the way home we had seen him, big and cinnamon-colored, likely a black bear in species but just possibly a grizzly. A forest ranger friend had said a grizzly sow with cubs had been seen in the drainage a few weeks earlier.

The boys and I had stopped the horses to peer, as best we could, through the partial screen of woods at the moving bear. The glimpses I did have showed a creature that exuded the presence of *Ursus horribilis*, the grizzly bear, and I've since believed it was that awesome animal we were watching. Jonathan and I planned strategy in whispers. At the first sign of the bear moving toward us, we would head the horses down the trail. The horses themselves had not caught a whiff, thus were calm, appreciative of the rest stop. Little Steve listened to Jon and me stoically. Then he said, "Haven't we watched enough?" Jon and I laughed under our breaths, and we spurred down the trail.

I would not see much wildlife today. The rain nearly blinded me, and the horses sensed home. We clipped along. The familiar, poetic names of the places we passed registered as I rode through the rain, Wounded Man Creek (its *other* fork, draining into the Stillwater), Roosevelt Lake, The Meadows, and then, nearly home, within reach of the most out-of-shape Sunday afternoon hikers, Sioux Charley Lake. Today's rain had defeated all hikers, so my horses and I had the trail to ourselves. Lunch was saddle-bag snacks, eaten standing next to Major and holding his reins in one hand. He was impatient now. This had been a good trip, but it was done now and he wanted the green, green grass of home.

And then we were there, the parking lot and its few cars surreal. Major looked at the cars and snorted, doing a sidestep spook as we passed them. Three days ago he had spooked at a moose. Now it was an object of civilization that seemed unusual and threatening to him.

Emily had delivered the pickup and horse trailer to the trailhead. Seeing them parked in the lot was a touch of home. I tied Major and Sugar to the trailer, unsaddled, and walked back to the trailhead signs. There was a warning posted that the Stillwater trail was impassable to horses just above where we had joined it at Horseshoe Creek. One of my alternative routes would not have worked.

Though anxious to go home, I now walk a short distance up the trail I have just ridden down. Right above the trailhead the valley is a rocky V through which the Stillwater River tumbles, froths, and pounds, the trail a ledge clinging to the side above the river. I walk to where the rocks vibrate from the river's assault. On small day hikes in the past, I've always considered this stretch of trail frightening, but it does not seem so now. I look up the rising trail until it disappears into the timber at the head of the chute. Then I go back to my vehicle, load the horses, and drive home.

# EPILOGUE

Like Thoreau's farmer who owned the farm but worked so hard on it he had no time to enjoy its beauties, writers sometimes spend so much time writing about things they love that they are not able to indulge in them. I know a senior editor of a major horse magazine who confessed she worked such long hours that she rarely had time to ride, that for several years now she has not been able to even have her own horse. And so, at the end of this very busy summer, much of which has been spent working on the book you have just finished, I regret a certain void—our family was unable to take its usual pack trip in the Beartooth Mountains.

Since Emily and I were able to go to Spain in June, we cannot cry too loudly. But I do fear some repercussions. Our summer pack trip is like compressed, solid fuel, stored to slowly burn later, warming us on those snowbound days of winter when the sun disappears at four in the afternoon. Melville's Ishmael, whenever it was "a damp, drizzly November" in his soul, when the blues were upon him, when thoughts of death preoccupied him, when surliness toward others surfaced, looked to the sea. I look to the mountains.

Those of us who are creatures of words are lucky, for reading and writing can act as serviceable substitutes for doing. But when substitutes will no longer serve, when words, too, run thin, it is time to make promises—promises to keep.

So next spring, when the snow breaks and the calves are born, when virgin leaves come onto the aspen trees and the elk shed their winter coats in patches, I will call Ralph, our cowboy farrier, to come and get the horses ready. There will be Rockytop, nearing his fifteenth birthday, but still a colt; Marauder the gentleman, black and quiet and huge; Major, who at four is already "Old Reliable"; and Emily's horse Sugar, high-headed, proud, athletic, who walks on a mountain trail as if passing in review by a judge's stand. There may also be two others, Jed, the colt I am starting, and Monty, Emily's project, who at three will be old enough to cut their mountain teeth carrying light packs. All of them will still have some winter hair but will be snorty, too long on oats and hay, ready to shake off cabin fever and go do something.

While Ralph shoes, I will dust off camp equipment and organize it into the manties and panniers. Then Emily and I and perhaps some friends will rendezvous at a trailhead I know well and leave the telephone behind for a few days. There will still be deadfall on the trail, so we will chop and saw our way to a clearing by a stream of roaring, milky, converted snow dashing down the mountain. In the tent will be the sheepherder's stove, and on it soon, a pot of coffee. What will we *do* there in camp? That is of almost no importance. We will be there.

And you should go too. There is adventure out there made better by the strength and willingness of a good horse. I hope, in some small way, this book has helped you find it.

# APPENDIX

The following companies offer one or more of the activities discussed in this book. Their specialties are noted in parentheses. The term *western variety* is used to indicate that many activities are offered, while the term *horseback vacations* means that riding activities are primary.

**ALASKA**

Lost Creek Ranch
Box 84334
Fairbanks, Alaska
907-672-3999
(pack trips)

**ARIZONA**

Adventure Guides, Inc.
7550 East McDonald Drive
Scottsdale, Arizona 82250
800-252-7899
(western variety)

Friendly Pines Camp
933-B Friendly Pines Road
Prescott, Arizona 86303
602-445-2128
(horseback vacations)

Hartman Outfitters
448 Lake Mary Road
Flagstaff, Arizona 86001
602-865-4777
(horseback vacations)

## CALIFORNIA

FITS Equestrian
685 Lateen Road, D-E
Solvang, California 93463
800-666-3487
(books foreign horseback treks)

Horn Fork Guides, Ltd.
Box 1030
Buena Vista, California 81211
719-395-2081
(pack trips)

Rainbow Pack Station
Box 1791
Bishop, California 93515
619-873-8877
(pack trips)

Red's Meadow Pack Outfits
Box 395
Mammoth Lakes, California
   93546
619-934-2345
(western variety)

Ricochet Ridge Ranch
24201 North Highway 1 (WH)
Fort Bragg, California 95437
707-964-7669
(horseback vacations)

Saddling South
4510 Silverado Trail
Calistoga, California 94515
707-942-4550
(pack trips and rides in Mexico)

## COLORADO

American Wilderness Experience
Box 1486
Boulder, Colorado 80306
800-444-0099
(western variety—books adventures throughout West)

Backcountry Outfitters
Box 4190
Pagosa Springs, Colorado
   81157
800-898-2006
(western variety)

C.R.C., Inc.
8464 Old San Isabel Road
Rye, Colorado 81069
719-489-2266
(working ranch vacations)

Diamond Lodge
2038 Sierra Verde Drive
Durango, Colorado 81301
303-259-9393
(horseback vacations)

Echo Canyon Guest Ranch
Box 328
La Veta, Colorado 81055
719-742-5524
(western variety)

Kelly Place
14663 County Road G
Cortez, Colorado 81321
303-565-3125
(wagon trains)

McNamara Ranch
Box 702
Florissant, Colorado 80816
719-748-3466
(working ranch vacations)

Rawah Guest Ranch
Fort Collins, Colorado
800-820-3152
(western variety)

Ryan's Roost
Box 218
Lake City, Colorado 81235
303-944-2339
(horseback vacations)

Sylvan Dale Ranch
2939 N.C.R. 31D
Loveland, Colorado 80538
303-667-3915
(western variety)

T Post Ranches
5127 County Road
Antonito, Colorado 81120
719-376-2136
(working ranch vacations)

Teocalli Outfitters
Box 1425
Crested Butte, Colorado 81224
303-349-5675
(pack trips)

The Cowhand Cattle Drives
Box 743
Woodland Park, Colorado
    80866
800-748-3837
(cattle drives)

Uncompahgre Outfitters
16011 Transfer Road
Olathe, Colorado 81425
800-423-1547
(western variety)

Welder Outfitting Services
Box 823
Meeker, Colorado 81641
303-878-4559
(pack trips)

Weminuche Wilderness
    Adventure
17754 C.R. 501
Bayfield, Colorado 81122
303-884-2555
(western variety)

Western Safari Ranch
Box 128
Fairplay, Colorado 80440
719-836-2431
(western variety)

## IDAHO

Granite Creek Guest Ranch
Box 340
Ririe, Idaho 83443
208-538-7140
(working ranch vacations)

Hidden Creek Ranch
7600 East Blue Lake Road,
    Dept. W2
Harrison, Idaho 83833
208-689-3209
(western variety)

McGarry Ranches
6140 West 5000 South
Rexburg, Idaho 83440
208-356-6531
(working ranch vacations)

Silver Spur Outfitter
Box 406
Dubois, Idaho 83423
208-374-5684
(working ranch vacations)

## KANSAS

L and L Lodge
RR2, Box 71
Concordia, Kansas 66901
913-243-1785
(western variety)

## MISSOURI

Cross Country Trail Ride
Box 15
Eminence, Missouri 65466
314-226-3492
(horseback vacations)

Golden Hills Ranch
Route 1, Box 55
Raymondville, Missouri 65555
800-874-1157
(horseback vacations)

Upper Jack's Fork Trail Rides
Route 2, Box 163
Summersville, Missouri 65571
417-932-4033
(horseback vacations, trail rides)

## MONTANA

63 Ranch
Box WH979
Livingston, Montana 59047
406-222-0570
(working ranch vacations)

Bear Creek Guest Ranch
Box 151
East Glacier Park, Montana
  59434
800-445-7379
(western variety)

Bear Paw Outfitters
Route 38, Box 2032
Livingston, Montana 59047
406-222-6642
(horseback vacations)

Beartooth Guest Ranch
Nye, Montana 59061
406-328-6194
(traditional guest ranch)

Boojum Expeditions
14543 Kelly Canyon Road
Bozeman, Montana 59715
406-587-0125
(books trips in China)

Bozeman Trail Camp, Inc.
Box 71
Pryor, Montana 59066
(working ranch vacations)

Castle Reef Cowgirl Camp
Box 86
Wisdom, Montana 59761
406-689-3183
(horseback vacations for girls)

Custer Country Wagon Trains
Box 543
Hardin, Montana 59034
(wagon trains)

Davis Creek Camp
Sarpy Route
Hysham, Montana 59038
406-342-5423
(western variety)

Grassy Mountain Ranch
Box C
Townsend, Montana 59644
406-547-3402
(horseback vacations)

Great Divide Guiding
Box 315
East Glacier Park, Montana
  59434
800-421-9687
(pack trips)

K Bar L Ranch
Box 287
Augusta, Montana 59410
406-689-3183
(western variety)

Lost Fork Ranch
11-12 Highway 287 North
Cameron, Montana 59720
406-682-7690
(western variety)

Montana Wilderness
  Experience
364 McCarthy Loop WH
Hamilton, Montana 59840
406-363-4129
(western variety)

Paintbrush Trails
Absarokee, Montana 59001
406-328-4158
(trail riding, pack trips)

Rainbow Outfitters
Box 494
Polaris, Montana 59746
406-834-3444
(western variety)

Stoney Lonesome Ranch
Box 37
Absarokee, Montana 59001
406-932-4452
(working ranch vacations)

The Johnson Place
Box 578
Absarokee, Montana 59001
406-328-4195
(horseback vacations)

The Tom Miner Lodge
Route 1, Box 660
Emigrant, Montana 59027
406-848-7525
(working ranch vacations)

Tongue River Wagon Trains
Box 432
Ashland, Montana 59003
800-345-5660
(wagon trains)

**NEBRASKA**
7 Springs Ranch
HC 54, Box 34
Kimball, Nebraska 69145
303-437-5345
(working ranch vacations)

**NEW MEXICO**
Copper Country Outfitters
Box 2333
Silver City, New Mexico 88062
505-388-2127
(pack trips)

**OHIO**
Riding Vacations, Inc.
Box 502A
Richfield, Ohio 44286
216-891-9325
(western variety)

**SOUTH DAKOTA**
Bunkhouse Bed 'n Breakfast
14630 Lower Spring Creek
  Road
Hermosa, South Dakota 57744
605-342-5462
(working ranch vacations)

Gunsel Horse Adventures
Box 1575
Rapid City, South Dakota
    57709
605-343-7608
(horseback vacations)


**TENNESSEE**
Bucksnort Trail Ride, Inc.
Box 329
Bortland, Tennessee 37148
615-325-2827
(horseback vacations)

Buffalo River Trail Ride
Box 591
Waynesboro, Tennessee 38485
615-722-9170
(western variety)

Xanadu Farm
Box 152
Triune, Tennessee 37014
615-395-4771
(horseback vacations)


**UTAH**
All 'Round Ranch
Box 153
Jensen, Utah 84035
800-603-8069
(horseback vacations)

Bar S Ranch
Box 332
Tabiona, Utah 84072
801-848-5667
(horseback vacations)

Dalton Gang Adventures
Box 8
Monticello, Utah 84535
801-587-2416
(working ranch vacations)

Ruby's Outlaw Trail Rides
Box 1
Bryce, Utah 84764
801-834-5265
(horseback vacations)

**VIRGINIA**
Hungry Horse Farm
Route 1, Box 316
Ivanhoe, Virginia 24350
703-744-3210
(horseback vacations, trail
    riding)

**VERMONT**
Mountain Top Inn and Resort
Box 582, Mountain Top Road
Chittenden, Vermont 05737
800-445-2100
(horseback vacations, trail
    riding)

**WISCONSIN**
Wilderness Pursuit
N5773 Reseswood Avenue
Neillsville, Wisconsin 54456
715-743-4484
(horseback vacations)

**WYOMING**
Bitterroot Ranch
Box 807
Dubois, Wyoming 82513
800-545-0019
(equestrian vacations)

Boulder Lake Lodge
Box 1100 H
Pinedale, Wyoming 82941
800-788-5401
(pack trips)

Box K Ranch
Box 110-W
Moran, Wyoming 83013
307-543-2407
(horseback vacations)

Castle Rock Ranch
412 County Road 6NS
Cody, Wyoming 82414
800-356-9965
(horseback vacations, trail
  riding)

Cheyenne River Ranch
1031 Steinle Road
Douglas, Wyoming 82633
307-358-2380
(cattle drives)

Darby Mountain Outfitters
Box 447
Big Piney, Wyoming 83113
307-386-9220
(western variety)

David Ranch
Box 5
Daniel, Wyoming 83115
307-859-8228
(working ranch vacations)

Equitour
Box 807
Dubois, Wyoming 82513
800-545-3363
(books riding treks worldwide)

Glen Eden Stables
Box 6150
Cheyenne, Wyoming 82003
303-846-1694
(horseback vacations)

Green River Outfitters
Box 727WH
Pinedale, Wyoming 82941
307-367-2416
(pack trips)

Schively Ranch
1062 Road 15, E-4
Lovell, Wyoming 82431
307-548-6688
(working ranch vacations)

Three Quarter Circle Ranch
Box 243-WH
Lander, Wyoming 82520
307-322-2995
(working ranch vacations)

Trails West, Inc.
65 Main Street
South Pass City, Wyoming
  82520
800-327-4052
(western variety)

Wagons West
Box 1156
Afton, Wyoming 83110
800-447-4711
(western variety)

Wiggins Fork Lodge
Box 562
Crowheart, Wyoming 82512
307-486-2269
(horseback vacations)

## AUSTRALIA

Bullock Mountain Homestead
Bullock Mountain
Glen Innes, Australia NSW
  2370
(horseback vacations)

## CANADA

Alberta Frontier Guiding
Box 83
Sundre, Alberta,
  Canada TOM 1X0
403-638-2897
(western variety)

Alberta Outfitters Association
Box 277
Caroline, Alberta,
  Canada TOM OMO
403-722-2692
(horseback vacations)

Boundary Ranch
Box 44
Kananaskis Village, Alberta,
  Canada TOL 2HO
403-591-7171
(pack trips)

Brewster Rock Mountain
Box 964, Caribou Street
Banff, Alberta,
  Canada TOL OCO
403-762-5454
(pack trips)

Flying U Ranch
Box 69
70 Mile House, British
  Columbia,
  Canada VOK 2KO
(western variety)

Ghost Wilderness Resort
Box 4069
Williams Lake, British
  Columbia,
  Canada V2G 2V2
604-398-1087
(horseback vacations)

Hank and Bobbi Peterson
Box 277
Caroline, Alberta,
  Canada TOM OMO
403-722-2692
(horseback vacations)

High Country Tourism
  Association
Department WH, #2-1490
  Pearson PL
Kamloops, British Columbia,
  Canada V1S 1J9
800-567-2275
(western variety)

Horseback Adventures Limited
Box 73
Brule, Alberta,
  Canada TOE OCO
403-865-4777
(horseback vacations)

Miette Trail Rides
Box 7622-W
Edson, Alberta
  Canada T7E 1V7
403-723-3380
(pack trips)

Rich Hobson Frontier Cattle
  Drives
Box 2552
Vanderhoof, British Columbia,
  Canada VOJ 3AO
604-567-4664
(cattle drives)

Saddle Peak Trail Rides
Box 1463
Cochrane, Alberta,
  Canada TOL OWO
403-932-3299
(western variety)

Three Bars Ranch
S.S.3, Site 19W, Box 62
Cranbrook, British Columbia,
  Canada VIC 6H3
604-426-5230
(western variety)

Warner Guide and Outfitters
Box 2280
Banff, Alberta,
  Canada TOL OCO
800-661-8352
(horseback vacations)

**FOREIGN TREK BOOKING
AGENTS**

Boojum Expeditions
14543 Kelly Canyon Road
Bozeman, Montana 59715
406-587-0125
(books treks in China)

Equitour
Box 807
Dubois, Wyoming 82513
800-545-3363
(books treks throughout world)

Saddling South
4510 Silverado Trail
Calistoga, California 94515
707-942-4550
(treks and pack trips in Mexico)

FITS Equestrian
685 Lateen Road, D-E
Solvang, California 93463
800-666-3487
(books treks throughout world)

# INDEX

**Page numbers in italics represent illustrations.**

Absaroka-Beartooth Wilderness Area (Montana), 142

Adams, Andy, 65, 68–72, 77–78

Adams, Nick (Hemingway character), 151–152

Alhambra, 104

Alpujarra Mountains, 100, 123

American West, 7, 9, 37, 58

Andalusia (Spain), 115

Andalusian, 101, 106, 108, 111

Appaloosa, 144

Arabian, 111, 126, 128

Austria, 111

"Bear, The," 138

Beartooth Highway (Montana/Wyoming), 138, 140

Beartooth Mountains, 100

Berchules (Spain), 113, 115, 116, 120–121

*Big Two-Hearted River*, 152

Bitterroot Ranch, 46–48

Black Elk, 6

Blackfeet Agency, 78

Bob Marshall Wilderness Area (Montana), 45

Bozeman, John, 62–64

Bozeman Trail, 55, 62, 64

Bridger, Jim, 63

Bridger-Teton National Forest, 62

bridle, 21–24

Brown, Mark, 63

Bubión (Spain), 105–106, 108, 121

Bull Mountains (Montana), 128

bullfight, 112

Bunkhouse Bed 'n Breakfast, 44

Cassidy, Butch, 3

Cheyenne, 5

Chief Gall, 6

cinch, 16–21, *22*

*City Slickers*, 76

Colorado, 104

competitive trail riding, 135

# Index

Connolly Brothers saddle, 21
Cooke City, Montana, 138
Costa Del Sol, 112, 122
"Cowhand Cattle Drives, The," 77
Crazy Horse, 7, 64
Crook (General), 6
Crow Tribe, 2, 6
Custer, General George Armstrong, 3–7, 64

Daisy Pass (Montana), 151
Day, Jim, 38
Decker pack saddle, 84–88, 96, 137
dehydration (in horses), 130–134
direct reining, 10
Drago, Harry Sinclair, 62
dressage, 125

Eaton brothers, 38–39
Eliot, T. S., 149
Emerson, Ralph Waldo, 30, 100
endurance riding, 126ff
Equitour, 46, 102–104, 122
*Equus*, 7
Erskine, Bess, 38

*Far West* (riverboat), 6
Faulkner, William, 138
FITS Equestrian, 122
forest fires, effects of, 148
Fox, Bayard, 46–48, 102–104

gaited horses, 12, 28
gaits of horses, 28
Golden Hills Trail Rides & Resort, 44
Granada (Spain), 104, 120–121
Grand Teton mountains, 60

grizzly bear, 145, 162

halter and haltering, 14ff
ham (of Andalusia), 118
Hanson, Kelly Klick, 45
Hedrick, Corky and Clarice, 48–51
Hemingway, Ernest, 104
horse, points of the (illustration), 11

Icelandic Pony, 28, 123
Idaho, 44

Johnson, Elmer, 28

K Bar L Ranch, 45
Keats, John, 100
Knighton, Cliff, 127
Knighton, Dr. Sue, 128ff
Kuralt, Charles, 140

latigo, 18, *22*
leg cues, 10
Little Bighorn River, 4
*Livingston Enterprise*, 38
*Log of a Cowboy, The*, 65, 68–72, 78
*Lonesome Dove*, 101–102
Love, Dallas, 99–123

Madrid (Spain), 104
manty, 87–88
Marsh, Captain, 6
"Master and Man," 57
Melville, Herman, 165
Mexican cowboy tradition, 9
Miller, George, 58–61
Missouri, 44
Missouri Fox Trotter, 28

Montana, 4, 35, 39, 45, 57–58, 65, 79, 99, 115
Moors, 104, 110, 116
Morab, 129
Morgan Horse, 128–129
Mormon trail, 55
mounting the horse, 24–25
mules, 80ff, 112, 127
Mulhacén, Mount (Spain), 118

Nebraska, 76–77
neck reining, 10, 26
North Dakota, 55

Oregon Trail, 55, 62
Oregon Trail, The, 106, 126
Orwell, George, 104
O.T.O. Ranch, 35–40
Outlaw Trail, 3

Paintbrush Trails, 81
panniers, 84–88
Parkman, Francis, 106
Paso Fino, 28
Percheron, 56, 60
Peruvian Paso, 28
Plainsmen of the Yellowstone, The, 63
Pride Piper, The (Tennessee Walking Horse stallion), 11–31
"Prisoner of the Caucasus, The," 127
Pony Express, 126
Pryor Mountains, 101

Quarter Horse, 129

Randall, Dick, 38
Red Cloud, 63–64

Roads to Empire, 62
Rocky Mountain Elk Foundation, 39–40
Roundup, Montana, 128

saddles, 16–21, 22
Santa Fe Trail, 55
sawbuck pack saddle, 84–88
Scotland, 100
7 Springs, 76–77
Seville (Spain), 112
Shane, 60
Sierra Nevada Mountains (Spain), 100
Silver Spur Outfitter, 44
Silvertip Ranch, 142–143
Sioux, 5, 63
Sitting Bull, 64
Slough Creek (Montana), 137ff
Smokey Bear, 148–149
Snake River, 62
South Dakota, 44
Spain, 10, 65, 84, 99–123
stallions (as saddle horses), 12
Stillwater River (Montana), 148ff
stirrup, 21
Stoney Lonesome Ranch, 48–51
Sun Also Rises, The, 118

tackaberry, 18, 22
tapaderos, 22, 33
Tennessee, 126
Tennessee Walking Horse, 2, 11, 28, 125, 128–129, 137, 139
Texas, 69
Thoreau, Henry David, 40–41, 165
Thoroughbreds, 128
three-day eventing, 125
Tolstoy, Leo, 57, 127

Index

Trevélez, Spain, 101, 109–114, 123
Twain, Mark, 34

U. S. Forest Service, 73, 144, 147

Veleta, Mount (Spain), 118
vet-chek, 130ff

Wilcox, Wanda, 81
wilderness safety, 145–147
Wolf Mountains, 3
Wyoming, 45, 60, 102

Yellowstone National Park, 38, 137–143